Living Normal in a Handicapped World

by

Pete Workman

authorHOUSE®

AuthorHouse™
1663 Liberty Drive, Suite 200
Bloomington, IN 47403
www.authorhouse.com
Phone: 1-800-839-8640

First published by AuthorHouse 8/20/2007

ISBN: 978-1-4343-1799-5 (sc)

Library of Congress Control Number: 2007903950

Printed in the United States of America
Bloomington, Indiana

This book is printed on acid-free paper.

Table of Contents

CHAPTER ONE

My Early Years

My parent's met in 1950 at a skating rink in Chattanooga. My dad was from Alabama and my mom was from North Carolina. They both worked for the same company. They met by chance. My dad noticed these young ladies standing alone and talking. He decided to show his moves on the floor and when he did, he busted his ass. The young ladies began to laugh but one in particular laughed harder than the rest. He returned to his feet and skated over to her and began a conversation. He found out that they worked at the same place. He asked her if she would like to go out with him on a date. She accepted. They dated for about 5 months then were married. Her father was furious. He did not attend the wedding. They bought a house in the eastern part of town. They both continued to work until mom was notified that she was with child. In 1954, they were graced with a son. The son was me. Mom did not quit work immediately. My aunt took care of me until she got married when I was about two. It was at this time my mom quit working. My parents realized that there might be something wrong with me physically because I kept falling down whenever I tried to walk. They took me to a doctor who ran tests. His diagnosis was that I had Cerebral Palsy in my right side. My parents were very upset. The doctor informed them that it was not fatal. It was a birth defect. It was like I had a stroke at birth. He also said I would walk with a limp and my strength in my right side would be limited. The doctor said my brain was as normal as any other child my own age. He said that I was most likely smarter than children much older than me. He said that I should be treated as a regular kid. My parents were glad that my brain was not effected by this birth defect. I was able to learn. I learned the alphabet when I was two and I could count.

The cars use to look different than they look now and if my dad asked me the type of car that had just passed us, I could tell him. My parents got me a record player and I was singing along with Elvis, carrying a tune.

My mom had another child a year and a half later, a girl. She was born without any defects except she did not like Santa Claus. She cried when mom tried to put her in his lap. I thought that was funny. In the early sixties mom had another child, also a girl. She was and is something else. All of the children in our family were treated the same. We were all loved a lot. We were not abused but we were spanked when we deserved a whipping. We were very lucky to have great parents.

We grew up in a great neighborhood. There were many children. There were more boys than girls but not by much. We played football in the fall, baseball in the summer and basketball in the winter. We camped out in the summer and roamed the neighborhoods at night. This was the time in America when fences did not exist in anyone's backyard. Our neighborhood had picnics in the summer and Christmas parties at Christmas. We all attended the same church. We all went to the same vacation bible school. We played sports during the day and car light monster at night. Four of the people that I grew up with are gone now but I still have my memories.

We bought some land on the west side of town when I was 14 because my dad decided that he did not want to live in the city. I had to make friends over again. I decided that having friends were more important than having good grades. My parents did not share the same feeling as I. I made good enough grades in high school to earn a vocational rehabilitation scholarship to any college in Tenn. I wanted to attend MTSU, however my dad wanted me to go to the college closest to home so I could live at home. He said if I still wanted to go to MTSU after my sophomore year then I could go. I said o.k. When the time came for me to transfer to MTSU he said that he spent the money on other things. I said fine. I quit school. This is something that I have regretted doing.

I went to work doing various jobs. I worked for a driving range and a finance company at the same time. I soon left the driving range because it interfered with my night life. I was the repo man for the finance company. Two separate times I thought I was going to die. The first was when I had to go to the poorer side of town to get a car from a black lady who had fallen three payments behind on her car. I knocked on her door and told her why I been sent by the loan company. She began to cry. I told her that I was sorry but

I had no choice. She gave me the keys and I walked out the door. Much to my surprise there were three black gentlemen sitting on my brand new car. They informed me that I could not remove her car from their neighborhood. I agreed with them and left. I went and found two police officers. We went back to the ladies apartment and picked up the car.

The other time I had phoned a man that I was coming to his place to repo his vehicle for not making his payments on his car. He said that when I arrived he would pay me 2 payments. When I got there, all he possessed was a six-pack in one hand and a 12 gauge in the other. He said if I tried to take his car then he was going to shoot me. I said fine, keep your car, and I left. I went to the local police station and they sent two officers with me to get the car. I not only got the car but the man went to jail.

I also spent some time working at a strip club in Nashville. I was the exotic janitor. This job was o.k. But not that exciting. I did meet some interesting people. I became friends with a biker gang. Their girlfriends worked at the strip club as dancers. They liked me for reasons I still cannot understand but they allowed me the chance to party with them. I enjoyed their company because I felt safe when I was with them. The authorities did not bother them. If a person was lucky enough to be able to hang around them, that person would be protected as long as you did not reveal what they did to make a living or mess with one of their women. I never asked how they got their money nor am I going to guess. I just know that they were a great bunch of guys.

When I worked at the seafood establishment, I performed different jobs. The most important job that I performed while working there they did not have to pay me. I sold drugs. I made more money doing this than the small pay check I received from them every week. We did play a lot of jokes on people especially the bosses. I remember this one boss from the north, a real asshole that I locked in the freezer for over an hour. After I let him out his glasses were completely frozen.

I had met a woman during 1979 and we started dating. We dated off and on through the years. Her dad finally asked what my intentions were towards his daughter. I said I would marry her if I could find a job. He said that he could get me an interview with a battery company in a small town outside of Chattanooga. I said that if I got the job I would ask his daughter to marry me.

I went home and told my parents that I was going to marry Carol. My mom was happy that I was finally going to marry and leave the nest. This event did not make my dad particularly happy. He told me that he did not like Carol nor did he trust her. My dad is a very smart man. He asked me what was in this marriage for me. I said that I would receive a job interview with a local battery company, but if I did not get the job there would be no marriage. He said that seemed fair. I asked him to be my best man at the wedding. He said that honor was usually to be given to your best friend. I told him that he was my best friend. He smiled and said o.k. I asked my grandpa if he would marry Carol and myself. He said that he would be glad to do the honors.

Carol's dad must have known that I would get the job because he began to make the arrangements for the wedding. He reserved the church ordered the flowers, reserved the club on the river for the reception, reserved the band and ordered the booze. I really believed that this marriage was the biggest mistake I have ever made in my entire life.

CHAPTER TWO

Life Before XYZ

My girlfriend's father was true to his word, he introduced me to the personnel director of XYZ Battery Company. We talked for a few minutes. He asked me if I had a high school degree and a college degree. I told him I was a high school graduate and that I attended college but grew tired of the grind and quit.

I told him about my physical handicap, but I knew if given a chance I could do the job. He said they were hiring for the summer, plus if I excelled I would be called back if there was a layoff. I again expressed I only wanted a chance. He sarcastically said if you passed the physical, I could have the job.

After I had our little chat, he arranged a physical for the next week with their doctor. I said o.k. and thanked him for talking to me.

My girlfriend's father and I went back to his house for dinner. He said that he had kept his part of the bargain, would I keep mine. I said if I got the job then I would keep mine. Looking back, I wished that I did not show up for the exam, but I did.

Surprisingly I passed. I told Mr. Jackson that I would ask his daughter to marry me.

I was to report to the main plant (there were two in that city) in the late spring for orientation.

I went home and told my parents I had gotten a job with XYZ Battery Company. They were excited. I said I was getting a job out of the deal with better than minimum wages and insurance benefits. Finally, with reservation dad gave his approval. Technically, I didn't need his approval, but I respected his opinion, and this made me happy.

Carol and I got married in May.

At the reception afterwards we partied all night. My baby sister got so drunk she fell off the toilet and broke the damn thing. My other sister fell into a potted plant. Everyone had a great time.

I think that was the only day out of two and a half years married to Carol that I was truly happy. The minute she said, "I do", she changed from Ms. Jekyll to Mrs. Hyde. I was so glad to go to work I thought I was on vacation eight hours a day. Dad was right she was just like her mother, a true bitch.

I began my job about three weeks after I was married. I started out on day shift. I thought I would be located there permanently. I was mistaken.

My job was putting bottoms of the cans of the lantern batteries. It wasn't a hard job, just boring. It took a week to get the hang of it. After awhile I got so far ahead, I could visit with my co-workers and make friends. All the people on the line were women. They were extra nice to me and I liked most of them. A few of them were special and I couldn't wait to talk with them. My boss was o.k., he had a dry sense of humor, but he could be an asshole if he wanted to be. I had a reasonably good time working on this line, but things were about to change.

At the end of the summer, my boss approached me and said that he needed to talk with me. I thought I was in trouble or about to be let go. I had worked all summer on day shift and I thought that I would remain on day's. I could not have been more wrong. He told me the company was transferring two people to the other plant and I was one. Looking back I wished that I had reacted differently. I got pissed. I had heard stories about the other plant, how dirty and noisy it was and I really did not want to go. I asked him why I had to go. He said that I had the lowest clock number. He said that he tried to stop my transfer. He could do nothing on my behalf. He said he had tried. I was so mad. I threw a box of batteries across the plant. Luckily, no one saw me do this because my ninety days were not in yet, and I could have been fired.

I showed up at plant (where batteries are made) the following Monday. I felt I had to start over. The jobs there were harder, but something soon happened that made my life a lot easier at least for a while.

Ralph, my new boss on day shift came to me and the other guy who had been transferred with me and stated that one of us had to go to second and the other to third shift. The other guy said he couldn't sleep during the day, so he preferred to go to second. I said I didn't care even though I had a better clock number. (The better clock number, the more senior your were.)

Ralph told us to report to our new shifts, for me that would be Sunday and the other guy would by Monday afternoon. After the meeting broke up Ralph told me I had gotten the better part of the deal because I would get twenty cents more an hour because the company thought that third shift was more stressful. Myself, I knew I would get more time away from Carol. I would be working while she was sleeping and be sleeping while she was working. I said to myself "there is a God and he likes me, he really likes me.

I reported to work the next Sunday night. I reported to my new boss – Red. He was a real son of a bitch and I thought he liked being one. He told me I was going to be cleaning the restrooms and taking out the boxes of trash to the compacter. He asked me if I thought I could handle it. I thought what a num-nut, but I said yes. He said he would be checking up on me often so I'd better be on my toes. I said if he had any suggestions to please tell me because I wanted to do the job correctly. I think I caught him off guard because he answered o.k. He told me to go up to the crib and meet the rest of the team. I did just that. I first met Annette and Ted. They had been working there for quite sometime and they knew the ropes. They also knew the shortcuts. Ted said he would help me for the first couple of nights but then I was on my own. Annette was a funny, decent looking divorcee who did not take shit from no one. She knew her job but she also knew her limitations. She was afraid of nothing. She always treated me with the utmost kindness unless I really screwed up, then she would put me in my place. Ted was a prankster. He would do his job as fast as he could and goof off the rest of the night. He was married to another bitch who stayed on his butt all the time. He also had a son. I think that was the reason he stayed married to her. He liked to work out a lot. He was weird sometimes but he was a good guy. We became good friends and still are today.

I finally got the handle on my job and even worked some overtime (more vacation time away from Carol). I also got into trouble from time to time. It was trivial stuff, but Red being the S.O.B. He enjoyed writing me up, I thought that he was proving that he was a better and more powerful person than I would ever be. Annette and Ted also got into trouble too. Yet they would tell Red what they thought of him, his family and his dog. I soon developed the same attitude.

December finally rolled around and a lot of people started hearing rumors of – dare I say it – a layoff. I knew if it happened, I could not do anything about it. The lowest clock numbers were laid off first. Usually rumors are 80% true. The layoffs did come and I was among them. The only thing that bothered me about the whole thing was I was going to be with Carol more than I wanted to be. They said the layoff would probably last until March. I would draw unemployment until then or I could try to find another job. I decided for the former because I knew I had done a decent job and I was the token handicap person, so I decided to hang out at the golf course and play when possible. I would try to rekindle the fire and passion that was missing from my marriage. (It didn't happen though).

This was the first time I would be laid off by XYZ (there would be quite a few more).

One thing I did realize was that I was not in love – or even like Carol. We separated for a while. I was going to file for divorce but my mom talked me out of it. Mom said marriage was sacred and it takes two people working as one to make it work. Stupidly, I took the advice. I do not mean to say my mom is stupid but she was totally wrong about Carol. She was a spoiled brat. If she couldn't afford an item, she would get a loan, mostly behind my back. Plus she was getting larger and larger even though she said she was dieting, yeah right and I'm the Pope. She was also doing more drugs. I gave them up (for the most part in my early twenties). I knew she was smoking a lot of pot, but also (even though I couldn't prove it) she was sniffing Cocaine. Her moods would change at a moments notice. She would bitch and gripe about anything and everything. That is enough about her. Even now, thinking about this time in my life makes me very depressed.

At this time, I need to backtrack and tell you about Leroy, my best friend. Who I first met at work. Ted had told him about me and since they (Annette, Ted and a few other people) were giving Leroy a birthday party at his apartment after work, I was invited to attend. I said sure. I went. Beer, alcohol was provided, as well as pot. Leroy had a very unique bong. I had never used one before, just smoking joints. Well to make this story short, he showed me how. Never stepping away from a new experience, I took a big hit. I wore dentures at that time, only the uppers. (I now have both the upper and lower). Well I started choking and when I coughed, my dentures flew out of my mouth clear across the room. Being so drunk and stoned, I just rose up from the couch walked across the room, wiped them off on my jeans and stuck them back into my mouth. Everyone laughed. Party continued.

I was called back to work in March to the packing plant doing the janitor's job with a fellow by the name of Ryan. I thought he was more different than anyone I had ever met. I thought he was crazy as hell but it turned out he was fairly intelligent. He said if we hurry up and do our work, we could take a nap back in the offices. Our boss was slow to catch on to things. He was very nervous about his numbers. Thinking he was going to be fired at anytime. Sometimes we would sneak up behind him and scare the shit out of him.

Ryan's girlfriend also worked for XYZ Battery Company so she would keep a watch out for Mr. Nervous. I got some of my best sleep during this time.

Leroy and Ryan were good friends, living on the same block. Leroy told me though not to trust Ryan because if it came down to me or him getting into trouble, Ryan would sell out. This bothered me. I told Ryan one night I was grateful to be working with a friend, he was quick to point out to me we were not friends but acquaintances. I was shocked and hurt. I told Ted what he said. He said do not worry about it, just be wary what you tell to certain people.

Ryan and I were not that close after that. I did learn a valuable lesson. I use to talk a lot but after that, I became a listener.

Leroy is more than just a friend to me; he's more like a brother. Everything I am he is not. I am older in years but he is older or should I say more mature about life and people.

When I first met Leroy, he was a ladies man. He played every sport he could. Racquetball, softball, snow skiing, skating, basketball, bowling and golf. I only played golf. He loved to go, take risks. Not I.

He came to XYZ Battery Company indirectly from the Army. He was stationed in Europe. He got married young, but the marriage didn't last. However it lasted long enough to produce a son. He is a fine kid. He lives in another state. Right now he is planning to go into business for himself.

Leroy really liked to go dancing and partying. I could write a book concerning him alone, and I do not know half the stuff that he has experienced. The common denominators between us were work and golf. We would leave work, go play until we were exhausted, go home, catch a few hours of sleep then go partying. We didn't go every weekend but at least twice a month. It really depended on his girlfriend at the time. He still likes to party though. I think it bothered him though he never let on that he couldn't beat me playing golf. He swung only with his arms. He finally took some lessons from a pro and he improved, I mean he really improved. The funny thing to me was the pro told him the same thing I had been telling him for years. I never asked him, but I wonder if he felt dumb!

About this time, Willie came back from the service and got his job back. If you went into the Armed Services while you were employed, when your stint was up, you not only got your position back, you kept your seniority.

Ted and Roscoe had just started playing golf with Leroy and me but they did not know the rules. The first time we went to play with them, I laughed and cried, then I got a little pissed. They drove their cart over the roped off areas and it took 5 ½ hours to play 18 holes. (For you non-golfers) that is about 1 ½ hours too long. When we finished Leroy and I told them when they learn the rules, they could play with us again. It took them about a month. They learned the rules. We let them resume playing with us again. This time we finished just under 4 hours. We began playing every Friday and sometimes during the week.

I stayed on third shift for the remaining of the year until December when I was, yes, you probably guessed it, laid off again. That night I had brought alcohol to work to give a drink to anyone that wanted one. I kept the bottles in my trash bin. I had bought some two liter Coke bottles and poured out half of the Coke then added bourbon and rum and also made a batch of screwdrivers. These bottles were empty by lunch break. This other guy had brought a bottle of Jack Daniel's and put it on the back dock where the trash compactors were located. By the time the shift was about over his boss had smelled liquor on his breath. The boss told him that if he showed him where he had hid the bottle he would not get into trouble and would be recalled when it was time to call people back. He said that he had put it on the back dock and his boss said for him to show him his hiding place. They went back to the dock and he said that he had placed the bottle behind some pallets. The bottle was not there. The man said that he did not move the bottle. His boss did not believe him. He was allowed to finish his shift. He was not called back. The bottle had been where the guy said he put it however I saw where he had place the bottle and after he had left for the last time that night I took it from behind the pallets and place it in my car. Those were the breaks and at XYZ Battery Company, I had to take my opportunities whenever they came. My friends and I thought we should have a lay-off party. It was a party that lasted 10 hours because the place we had rented was having another party that evening.

We had to bring our own liquor or drugs because we worked in a dry county – well sort of. They sold beer. However since I didn't drink beer, I had brought my own. We had such a great time. Someone had brought food and the jukebox was fixed so we didn't have to put in money. I got so drunk; I passed out about 3:30. In the meantime, Leroy and several others had gone to rent a room so they could party on. I woke up sometime later and found myself alone. I decided to go home. I think I fell down the stairs because I hurt so much the next day. Leroy told me on Monday that he had returned to find me missing. I had probably been better off if I had been killed because Carol was really pissed at me for being late. I got to work through shutdown (that's when they repair their outdated equipment and make a somewhat crappy attempt to do some housecleaning and painting etc.)

I received my call back notice in February. I was supposed to report to the powder room to do the laundry. I really liked that job. I also respected my stupidvisor Jere. He wouldn't ask you to do anything that he wouldn't do himself. He noticed in my file that I seemed to have an attendance problem. He said that if I could go six months without being tardy or missing a day, I would get a jacket from work, along with my attendance rating improving. I accepted the challenge. I accomplished this task and, true to his word, I received a nice windbreaker (black and yellow) with the company logo on the front. (However, someone stole the jacket from me about a month later).

I stayed on second shift for about 9 months. An opening came up on third shift, again in the janitorial field and I was the lowest clock number to bid so I got my old job back. I had to work with two older ladies, so I stayed to myself. I did my job o.k., just good enough to stay out of trouble. Come December we had another layoff, my last one.

On a personal note, Carol finally got sick of me, thank god. She said her mother caught me with another woman. She said we were wrapped in an exotic embrace. She (the mother) was partly correct. I was with a woman from work, and she had been having some personal problems. She started crying so I gave her a hug and informed her things would get better. That's what her mother saw. Carol and I agreed that we split everything evenly, right down the middle. Wrong. After she had discussed this matter with her mother, they got an attorney and informed me that she was filing for divorce because I had committed adultery. I said fine, I would counterfile because she and her brother were not only growing pot in our attic but were also selling drugs out of his apartment. She changed her tune damn quick. She filed for divorce due to irreconcilable differences. This is where I made a huge, huge mistake. I just wanted this three years of terror over – I really did get the shaft. I did not get an attorney. People let me stop right here and say if for some reason you no longer want to be with your spouse, please get a lawyer. She got everything except the bills. She kept the American Express card (because it's paid monthly). She even got the couch my mother gave me. All I got was a recliner, a T.V. And a debt for $15,000.00. At the time, I didn't care. She was out of my life. I had to file bankruptcy so I could set up a payment plan. I paid it off in about 6 years. They took the money out of my check. I closed the book on that chapter of my life.

I returned to work in the spring because we had some batteries (about a million) that were leaking and they needed people to sort the good from the bad. They informed us to take our time and like good little soldiers we did. It took about 3 months to do this project. Just as we finished we were all called back to work.

XYZ Batteries had another layoff, yet I wasn't included in this one, finally enough people had been hired so I had enough seniority to stick around. However, we did have another layoff party. It lasted 24 hours.

Some funny things did happen at the party. Ted mixed liquor with beer and started barfing out of the hotel suite into the swimming pool. He started feeling better when Leroy asked him if he wanted some pizza and poor Ted got sick again. The funniest thing that happened was that we had asked a girl named Aster to attend the party. She asked if sex was involved and I said "not to my knowledge". She said she would not come if sex was involved in any way. Sex was present at the party and she was the director of all sexual activities. She did everyone in the bathroom who was willing except Ted, Leroy and I and maybe some of the women.

When management figured out I could do the job and it received a bump in pay, ladies did not want it because they felt that they did enough cleaning at home and decided that I was having too much fun and the job was easier than the job they were doing,they decided that they wanted my job and eventually got it! They did not realize that I had done the job for about three years.

I knew how to do the job quickly and I worked with a partner who worked as hard as I did. We got through faster. After we had finished our work then we relaxed. Our jobs were put up for bid these ladies bumped us from the janitorial service. They did not find the job as easy. The women found out the work was harder than they thought. One of them came over to me to find out the secret. I told her that she and her partner needed to work together and the job would go by faster. She said that she did not like the person that she was working with, that she was a snob. I said then they had a problem because unless the two people did not work together, then the job would be harder. She said that she would tell the other lady how we got done with our work so fast. They never did work as a team. They barely finished their work before the shift was over. One of the ladies bid out of the job as soon as she could (a person had to wait six months before bidding on another job, another stupid rule).

The fellow that I had been working in the janitor service was a good guy. I told him one night that it was better working with a friend than someone I did not like. He calmly told me we were not friends but only acquaintances. This upset me very much. I told Leroy what he had said to me. He told me not to let it bother me because the man was strange. It was his loss not my loss. We continued to work together but spent our spare time apart. When we were bumped from our jobs and moved to second shift, he said that he was going to quit. I told him that he was nuts to walk away from a job that he had been doing for 10 years. I said that he would be making the same money and any job in the plant was not that hard. He said that he needed a change. He quit because he would have to work second shift. The funny thing was he said that the company would miss him. They did not miss him even a little. I think the company was glad that he was gone.

I started my new job on second shift working with a very nice woman name of Sally. She was the material handler on a line helping her load boxes onto a pallet for shipping. I was not very fast at first but got faster with time. Sally and I got along real well. I do not think I ever saw her not wearing a smile. We finished the project in the time we had to finish. Good for me because all my years of using drugs finally gotten the best of me. I went to the personnel director and told him that I had a drug problem. He asked me what kind of drugs I was using. I told him "speed". I used them at night while I had been working thirds but when I started working seconds I could not sleep. He said it was a good thing that I had come to him because if the company had caught me then I would have been fired. He said he would get into a treatment program as soon as possible. I had told him on Monday and by Thursday, I was on my way to a treatment center in Georgia. I decided that since this was my last chance to party, I drank a bottle of Bourbon on the way down to the center. Once I arrived, I discovered that an old friend from high school was in charge of the center. I found out that I would be there for 28 days. I did not tell my parents where I was for two weeks. I did contact my mom and told her where I was and why. She started to cry. I told her I had not lost my job and that I was getting clean. I also told her that I was receiving a paycheck. This news seemed to calm her down. I promised to call her the next weekend. She asked how long would I be staying. I said a month. She asked if

I needed anything and I said no thanks. After my treatment, I was drug free though the first few weeks were hard because I was very dependant on the drugs. I recovered very quickly after the effects of the drugs had subsided I returned to my original self. I made a promise that I would not use drugs any more unless under a doctors care. I would like to say that it took me about six months to eat chicken again because that is all the meat that they served. I learned ninety different ways to have chicken fixed for the patients. I was glad that I was going to return to work. I found out that I would have to attend meetings for a year and my blood would be monitored often to see if I was staying straight. XYZ Battery Company returned me to third shift so I could attend the meetings.

I started on a line helping a lady work on an automatic-packing machine. I liked the job. It was easy and it gave me someone to talk with that made the nights faster.

One night I had to run a packing machine alone. The other lady had help. I thought that particular night would never end, but when the night was over my boss said I had done an excellent job. About a month later, the packing machines had only one operator. Packing the boxes, still receiving the same pay rate I had been earning as a janitor.

I stayed on this job off and on until I lost my job (this will be covered in a later chapter.)

CHAPTER THREE

Rules

When I first went to orientation, they cover a set of regulations or rules that we needed to go by. Failure to abide by these rules could result in a write up or suspension or ultimately dismissal (in other words, you would be fired). Those rules scared the living hell out of everyone. As time passed however, the people settled into their jobs. We knew that the rules existed but we soon learned that the same rules did not apply to everybody.

RULE #1

Everybody had to be back to their work station when the bell rang during ten-minute breaks and lunch. Wrong. It depended on his or her seniority. The new people had to back on time, even if that meant you had to sit or stand until the others returned. The older people showed up at their own convenience.

RULE #2

Never and I mean never be away from your work station unless you are at break, lunch or need to go to the restroom. Now I have to admit I broke this rule quite often. When I was on the lantern line and I was way ahead, I would check on the ladies to make sure they had enough cans and if they did, I would go to the restroom and smoke a cigarette or go talk to a friend for a few minutes. (Smoking was permitted in the restroom and break rooms at this time). A lot of people broke that particular rule because it wasn't enforced too hard, unless you did (break the rule) too openly. One had to be coy but if one played his cards right, you could get away with rather easily.

RULE #3

A. No dating between a Stupidvisor and a regular employee at anytime. Ha! Ha! Ha! This happen so much, I began to think it was the company's sport. Every Stupidvisor had his or her own set of groupies. I referred to them as his or her herd of potential women or men that sometime down the road they could and most likely have sex. Most of the Stupidvisors that I knew, did not participate in this activity because they were dedicated family men or women but there were Stupidvisors that did. They held jobs over these people's heads. If you think about this the rule itself would be stupid, but I heard that there would be no exceptions for anybody including management. That's a laugh. As far as management was concerned if they made it to work, they were 90% through the day. The company could run itself without stupidvisors period. Stupidvisors were like camp counselors that use to keep an eye on the campers during the day and listen to the tattle-tales on each shift. They were there to settle disputes, write up people who flagrantly broke the rules, and turning in the best numbers of their lines.

B. No employee can date an opposite sex employee that is married. Ha! Ha! Ha! Not true! Here again I can truly say I did not abide by this rule myself. (I'll cover my story in another chapter). Affairs were almost a daily thing. Some were more out in the open. Most of the older employee's hobby was gossip. If you wanted to know about who is boppin' whom, all you had to do was go ask one of them. I think they should have started a company news letter for each plant and just distributed it and maybe even charge a quarter. They could have retired earlier than they did. Affairs were like a sport. Some people would have sex, at lunch, especially having a quick one. This rule wasn't enforced too much either. Management figured out than men and women working closely together, affairs were going to happen. The only time management became involved was when a spouse complained or thought his or her special other was foolin' around; then they would step in and bring the participating parties into their office and either tell them to be more discrete or stop all together. If they continued to see each other and the spouse complained again, then both parties would lose their jobs. As far as I know, a spouse complained only a few times. This even concerned management, if a Stupidvisor was caught messing around with a married employee just once, even if the spouse does not complain, he is fired while the employee kept his or her jobs. Management wished that this would not happen but they realized they were dealing with human beings and anything could and would most likely happen. I remember this one woman that we called "deep and wide" for obvious reasons, who took her boyfriends out to the parking lot during lunch for a quickie. Everyone knew what was going on because we would sit outside and watch the van bounce up and down. She was providing unknown entertainment for lots of people. She eventually was found out and she was let go.

RULE #4

The employee will never report to work under the influence of drugs or alcohol. What a big pile of shit that was. In the late eighties, you could have run a blood test on everyone, with exception for a few religious zealots and have to replace the whole lot. There were some on first and second shift too. Liquor, uppers, downers, coke, pot and beer was consumed before and during work. That is the only way some people could make it through their shift. I took uppers for a while but I quit in '89 only because I went through rehab.

I remember that in early '91 a friend of mine was plastered when he showed for work. We still used time clocks then and there was a pole right by the lantern line, and her walked right into the pole. He rose quickly thinking no one had seen what he had done. He turned around and saw two other guys and myself laughing our asses off. Everyone working that night knew that Chad was drunk or high, even the boss. She was a pain in the ass. She had her pets and Chad was probably her favorite. She let him return home sick. The funny thing to me was that Chad had to walk home, and was stopped by the police and they took him home after he convinced them he was sick not intoxicated. If it had been me, she would have suspended me on the spot, which would have led to my dismissal. I also had a Stupidvisor accuse me of coming to work drunk, because he could smell beer on my breath. I expressed to him I did not come to work drunk but I did not drink beer that often. I told him to check with me the next day and thing's might be different. I knew the person. He was talking about a friend. If there was, one thing I did learn is you do not squeal on other people. If you do you are not trusted your friends will dry up and you'll be alone. I found out my dad had something to do with his termination from his textile job in another city. He was arm wrestling when he was supposed to be working. Dad told me not to trust him and get away from him as soon as possible. I did just that.

No drinking or doing drugs on the job, but there were plenty of people smoking pot in the parking lot during break and lunch. I participated sometimes myself. The employees had to sneak and do things, but not management.

Except for Christmas when the rest of the packing plant was preparing for shut-down the Stupidvisors and most of the regular management would go to the front offices and getting blasted. This was o.k. to them. However, I could tell when some of the Stupidvisors had been drinking, because of the big mood swings, mostly bad, which took place during the last day of the week.

This event probably happened at both plants. However I cannot prove this but they knew it was going on. If they did not know, they would not do anything either. No, they were above reproach. I think they believed they (management) had the power, and they could do just about anything they wanted.

RULE #5

XYZ did not like any rabble-rousers, smartasses, troublemakers and non-union. We, as employees we were paid a fair wage and had good medical and dental benefits. We didn't need or want a union. I was anti-union. Other than that I was considered a troublemaker and smartass especially with Stupidvisors.

I made the mistake when I hired in with XYZ Battery Company that I would act stupid and ignorant because I didn't want them to know how intelligent I really was. I have a higher than average I.Q. Especially about history, science, government, music, and sports. Hell, I did not know or care how batteries were made the first 8 years I worked there.

Employees had really mess up before they were fired, like destroy or steal company property. Hit a Stupidvisor, neglect your job, causing production to go down or getting into a fight causing bodily harm to someone. Other that these things an employee could get away with almost anything.

Stupidvisors did not like employees to talk back to them about a job they had assigned you to do. If I thought a job could be done better, I just did the job the way I thought it ought to be done unless the Stupidvisor was nearby, then I would do it his way. Either way the job was getting done, and the Stupidvisor took all the credit. One thing an employee learned was that they shouldn't embarrass their Stupidvisors in front of higher management. When they impressed their boss that made them happy and they would usually passed on down to the employee their happiness by staying off your back. An employee should not show up the Stupidvisor because if this made him look like he was not doing his job, the trouble the employer could and most likely receive would come to him or her tenfold.

RULE #6

Each employee would be treated the same – no different that anyone else. Not true! Every Stupidvisor had their favorites – no exceptions on every shift. Employees, most always wanted to have a good relationship with their boss. Some even went so far as to perfect the art of kissing ass. Then there were the people I always thought of as the "Hitler Youth". They would tell on an employee to better their standing whether what they were saying was true or not. These people became people I, like many others stayed far away from. If people considered you a troublemaker, back-talker, or smartass your days were numbered.

I had a bad habit of telling people exactly what I thought. I was brought up thinking if your opinion or idea was better than someone was giving, then you expressed your idea. I finally learned that around most people, I should keep my mouth shut. If an employee ever got on a bosses bad side, it would be in that employee's best interest to move on, go to another shift or even sometimes change jobs and quit XYZ and move on with their lives. Sometimes an employee got lucky and the Stupidvisor was promoted or even moved to another plant. That often happened. If that occurred the ass-kissers and the "Hitler Youth" had to start over with their gossip and lies. The trick was to get to the boss first and pretend you were his closest ally. It does not sound like much, but it worked. It was a dog eat dog world and someone who was handicapped had to use whatever means she possessed to get by.

Stupidvisors did have their pets, so if you were friendly with one you needed to use that to your advantage.

I usually played golf to my bosses, giving them lessons to improve their golf games. This helped me on the job.

Golf was the company sport. If you were any good, that improved your standing with management significantly. Any time management came to me with a problem about golf I would try and help them.

Before we were bought by the latest owner we had company golf outings, which gave the employee's a day to be on an even plain with management. We were treated as equals. It was a four man select-shot. Everything was fairway including the rough. We had cash prizes and trophies for the winning teams and a crying towel for the team that finished last. We had a dinner afterwards. It was a great day, but things would return to normal the following Monday. I mean management would pretend that they did not know you or not remember you at all.

I began hanging around people like me. The people who either played golf or were troublemakers, smart asses, smart mouths or just primarily disregarded authority. I fit in well with these people. I thought they were cool. We did not take any shit from anyone. The ass-kissers were afraid of us because if they told on us for doing something which would improve their standing, when they left for break or lunch, we would make their job that much harder. They learned the hard way.

RULE #7

Every employee whether you were black, white, yellow or red would have to follow the same rules. This included your religious beliefs, male or female, politics or sexual orientation. This rule should never have even been in the book. You must understand I had never been a racist, but certain people got away with more than other employees. A person who wore the confederate flag on their t-shirt had to go home and change that shirt, but if another employee wore a Malcolm X hat or black softball league shirt to work, and someone complained the person was told to shut-up and get back to work. I have to say that was not exactly right. This left a lot of people bitter. This did not go over too well but nothing ever happened if a person complained about the situation. Little things cropped up now and then. Most of the people just let it go including myself.

The incident I would like to discuss at this time is about a gay employee and an acquaintance of mine. Everyone knew that homosexuals worked at XYZ Battery Company. They were not bothered at work. Most people even liked them. They did their jobs. Their sexual preference was well known, but never discussed. Anyway, a straight employee, Houston, was harassing the gay employee, George. Houston kept referring to George as a queer, fudge packer, bareback buddy and faggot. This went on for some time. It finally got so bad for George that he went to management about the problem. He said it was interfering with his job. Management brought Houston into the office and said the remarks had to stop immediately. He said he would stop. He did stop briefly, but he started his routine again, making sure there were no witnesses. As long as George had no witnesses it was just his opinion against Houston. Since his (Houston's) mother was a Stupidvisor, he was given some leeway.

Just when things had quieten down Houston made a huge mistake. George was going to his car, Houston hollered across the parking lot, see ya faggot. People heard that remark and reported it to management. Now George had his evidence. Houston found himself in big trouble. Nothing his mom could do. He had overstepped the line. He was fired on the spot. There are certain lines an employee can not cross and Houston crossed it.

There were certain words you could not say in mixed company, whether it was a man and women, black and white, and Stupidvisors and employees. The main words like whore, slut, whitey, cracker the "n" word, spear chucker, tar baby, and janitor-in-a-drum. I could go on but you get the idea. There are other little rules but I think I covered the major ones. Management have added some new rules, such as no smoking in the plant at all, random drug testing which was never enforced unless and employee had an accident etc.

As long as an employee followed these rules, things went fine. A person who was getting out of hand, causing trouble and the employee would have hell to pay or lose their job.

RULE #8

Management will always let an employee know in advance, no later than Wednesday if he or she had to work on Friday night or Saturday. This rule never actually existed. I stopped making plans for the weekend after I received tenure, even though I did not have to work overtime as much because of my disability. Sometimes I wanted overtime because I might be taking a trip. I received enough overtime when I was working as a janitor, but once I reach the floor I hardly got overtime at all, because the other employees would complain. They said I was taking away all the easy jobs and that they were stuck with the harder ones.

One girl who I will call Lassie was talking on my line and said since I was a cripple, I should not be working overtime on some lines because I took their resting jobs away. She said this "pleasant remark" directly in front of me. Now I'm not a tattle-tale, or a snitch. If I went to the office, it was because I had to. I might not have done a job incorrectly or to their satisfaction or I pissed someone off by saying something like, stop action like a baby or grow up or shut the fuck up or eat me – plainly it was my mouth. I could hurt someone's feeling at the drop of a hat, especially those women who carried their hearts on their sleeves or in their hands. Anyway I went to the numero uno of bosses, head over my bosses bosses' head, straight to the plant foreman whom I will call Noah. I said Lassie called me a cripple and I wanted something done about it. I told him if I had called her an ugly, fat, thumb sucking bitch I probably be suspended or fired. He said this was true and he would do something on my behalf. If he did do anything except talk to my boss and tell him, her kind of language would not be tolerated, and if it happened to me again, the party would be written up. The funny thing was nothing was said to her directly, Ted said it to a group of people. (I thought Ted had a crush on her and I was correct in my thinking, because they are living together now.) I returned to Noah's office and asked him that this was all he intended to do, that anyone could call me a cripple a gimp and a retard and nothing would happen to these people. He said Ted was supposed to talk to her directly. I said this was a crock of shit and that I could go to Vegas and place a bet that I would never complain to him about anything as long as I lived. I also would not volunteer for overtime if I were starving to death, or even living in my car. He said he was sorry I felt that way. I mumbled, "fuck you" and walked away. I never complained to management again. If I had a gripe, I would tell my Stupidvisor.

Anyway, most people had to wait to Thursday night or Friday to see if they had to work on Friday night or Saturday. It was done this way. 1. Volunteers and 2. By clock number. If you were getting married and you had a high clock number, the employee would have to take a vacation day just to be off. If they were drastic they could phone in sick, but this rarely happened because if you made the call, you would be charged with a day and a half absence because you got paid time and a ½.

Like I already stated the rest of the rules were minor, and if you had half a brain, you could get around them or use them to your advantage. XYZ Battery Management were not as smart as they thought they were and I will cover that in the next chapter. I figured out as each year went along, if one played their cards right, to coin a cliché, one could get away with almost anything and I <u>did</u>.

CHAPTER FOUR

Management

Management at XYZ Battery Company are an odd group of people. They remind me of the Nazi Party. They want people to follow their principles without following them theirselves. My first day of work management wore ties, the old-timers referred to them as shirts.

I am not saying that management did not like any particular group of people. Race religious group or sexual orientation did not matter to these people. Management did not like anyone except management.

Management acted as if they were in charge because it was their destiny. They felt it was their God given right to take two hour lunch breaks and report to work whenever they felt like showing up. If a third shifter had a complaint or a problem, they would sometimes have to wait an hour. Management actually did work from time to time but they made up for it later. They acted like a God – not the God. They would sit on Mount Olympus and grant favors to employees who had deserved them.

Management consisted of both Plant Managers, Personnel Manager any person that worked in the front office the company, Nurse and the Engineers both electrical and mechanical.

Then there is middle management who are in charge of the stupidvisors. We did consider the stupidvisors management. They were more like the police department or as I referred to them as the "gestapo".

Management had a pipeline of informants who kept close watch of any development, good or bad. These people were the professional ass-kissers. The employee who would sell his soul to improve their standing with the company. The employee would receive special compensation for the information if the information proved correct.

Most of the other employees never saw any management unless trouble came or jobs were being placed on the board for bid or on a special occasion.

Management would never talk to an employee unless they had to. For example if they were asked a question that concerned important information; dirt which they needed from a snitch. Most management walked through the plant because of boredom.

At Christmas time the Personnel Manager would go to each plant dressed as Santa Claus (he was the only person who could wear the suit). He would give out token gifts and candy. The Plant Manager would come to our plant when we had a pizza party because we had great production in a particular month.

Most of the management team was not worth a plug nickel. There was one an exception, at least to me. She was an assistant in personnel. I really respected her. I liked and trusted her. She did not fit the management stereotype at the company. She would not stab you in the back. I have heard other people say different but I do not believe this to be true. "Rita" had a great personality. She would help me with a problem, no matter the importance of the situation. I considered her my friend. I use to go see her sometimes to only talk. She understood my situation and she helped me through some tough times.

I will give an example of her helpfulness on my behalf. I had a Stupidvisor named "Jonah". He knew that I played golf. He knew that I was good but that I also had Cerebral Palsy. Before the shift ended, he asked me to play golf after work. I told him that I had not planned to play that day but he insisted. I said that I would meet him at the golf course an hour after work. I went home and told my wife that "Jonah" wanted me to play golf with him. "Alice" said that was fine with her and I went to the golf course. He got there and we began to play. I realized very quickly he was not very good. I think he shot 125 and I shot 75. When we finished I told him the areas that he needed to work on to improve his game. I really should have told him to take two weeks off and then quit. I think his golf game would have gotten a lot better. I did not realize that he got mad at me for beating him as bad as I did. I was very tired so I went home.

The next work night was Sunday. I discovered that my line was not going to run that night. I asked "Jonah" what I was going to do. He said that I would be packing on the line by hand. I told him that was impossible because of my disability. I also said that I was not fast enough and that I could not keep up with the other packers. He said that if I could play golf as well as did I should not have any problem packing batteries. I said that when I play golf I use different muscles and besides that I play or practice all the time. I said that you could be better if you played more than once a month. I even held up my hands and wiggled my fingers, my left hand was as good as his but my right hand was not.

A crowd had started to gather to hear the discussion, which turned into an argument. He said that if I did not pack I would have to go home. I told him no way that it was in my personnel file that I did not have to pack. The argument continued until I was very upset especially since he insisted that I go home. He finally said that I go to the break room. I started to go to the break room but I decided to call "Rita". I told her what had happened and that he was still threatening to send me home. She said not to worry. She asked me if he was near-by. He walked into the office and I told her that he was here. She said to go to the break room and wait for him to come to get me. She also said that she would be at the packing plant in the morning. She said for me to hand him the telephone and leave the office. I handed him the telephone and he asked who was on the line. I said that it was "Rita". His face turned white as a sheet. I smiled and left. "Jonah" came to the break room a little while later and told me to go take jackets off bad batteries. He said that I should not have telephoned "Rita". He said that I would be in trouble tomorrow and I told him that we would see who is in trouble. I went on to my job of the night. "Jonah's" boss came to work an hour early and called "Jonah" to his office. He came to where I was working and told me not to leave when the shift was over. I said I would stay for the meeting. He said that I did not have to clock out and I said that I did not intend to attend the meeting off the clock. The meeting began at 8:00. The people at the meeting were "Jonah", "Rita", two other bosses and me. "Rita" was very unhappy. I told her that I was sorry for calling her as late as I did but I could not think of anything to do. She said it was no problem and that she was sorry that last night's events occurred. "Rita" listened to both sides of the story even though she knew of my handicap. "Jonah" said that since I was so good at golf he felt that I should have the ability to pack batteries. When I challenged him and a crowd began to gather, he lost his head and he decided to show everybody who was in charge. When his bosses heard him repeat those words, they just lower their heads. The room got quiet. A hair could have fallen from someone's head and you could hear it hitting the floor. "Rita" said again she was sorry that the events ever occurred. She then asked "Jonah's" bosses why he did not know about my handicap. They said that they believed they had told him that the information was in my file. I believe that they hung him out to dry to cover their own butts. She told me that I had a job with XYZ Battery Company as long as I wanted a job. She told "Jonah" to apologize to me and mean it. She said that I could bring disciplinary action against "Jonah". That was a good idea and I was madder than hell but I just wanted the problem to vanish. I also wanted every boss who I would work with in the future to be made aware of my problem. I said that was all that I had to say but I did tell everybody in attendance that I had told him the information about my condition was in my file and if he had taken time to look, this would never had happened. I was told that I could leave and to close the door behind me. I said thank-you then left. Everyone else had to stay. I closed the door behind me but instead of leaving I listened at the door for a few minutes.

She told him that he was lucky that he still had a job. She said that I could have filed a complaint that would have been costly to the company. He would receive a write-up that would be placed in his file. She was still talking to him but I was satisfied, so I left. When I got outside, I found a lot of my friends waiting to find out what had transpired. I told them that the problem was fixed. They wanted details but I told them I could not talk about the meeting. I went home. My wife asked me what happened and I told her. She said I should have filed a complaint. I said that I thought I had handled it the right way because if I filed a complaint it could hurt me later. Looking back I guess I should have filed a complaint because of the way things turned out. "Rita" is no longer with the company. I think her husband was transferred. I heard she had a child. I hope she is doing fine. Look up class in the dictionary and you will see her picture. I miss talking with her. She was a good friend to me. I hope she is doing well.

We had a plant manager that we referred to as "Pretty Boy". That is what we called him behind his back. I do not remember his name but for this book, it really does not matter. He really thought he was so good looking. He dressed like a Mafia Don. He looked out of place. He was always trying very hard to impress people, especially the women. He was short but he strutted around as if he was a very big man. I never saw him talk to anyone on the plant floor but I really do not know because I was on another shift. He worked out with weights and had a very small waist line. His golf game stunk because he was too stiff. Once or twice, he came to our shift to see how things were going. He tried to sneak in without anyone knowing but the guard would always tip off the Stupidvisor and we would look busy. He never figured out how we knew he was there. He would walk around the plant, speaking to the company snitches and then leave. After he had gone, everything would get back to normal.

Most of management were ass-holes, at least during my time with XYZ Battery Company. They would say one thing to your face and then do the exact opposite thing that they had said in the first place. I really think that a person to work in management they had to fulfill two requirements: 1. They had to have a college degree and 2. They had to take a course on lying with a smile on your face. A person that could do this was a shoo-in for the job. I can honestly say that some of the best liars in the world worked for XYZ Battery Company.

They did have their stupid times too.

For an example, an engineer had made blue prints for a machine that would fit in a certain space. He had worked hard on the plans and when he finished the plans and he gave them to a boss so the boss and the mechanics could install the machine. The people who was trying to install the machine were confused. After studying the plans carefully, they came up with a solution. The people that were installing the machine realized that the plans were backwards to the space that they were given to place the machine. They had been trying to fit a square box into a round hole. They returned the plans to the engineer for correction but he did not find anything wrong with them. He returned the plans without making changes because he did not see anything to correct. The boss just reversed the plans to fix the space and installed the machine. I do not need to say this but I will, the engineer left the company soon after this happened.

Another example was that someone in management had a bright idea to put carpet in the offices of middle management. This did not seem to be a bad idea because it did make the offices look better. Every time that I think about this event I have to laugh. In order for the reader to have a better understanding of my amusement I need to explain that a battery floor is filthy. No matter how hard a person tries to keep their area clean, it is impossible. This dust gets on your clothes, body and covers the soles of a person's shoes. The floor is black all the time. Middle management is on the floor all of the time during the day.

My boss Saul and I just about fainted. When we saw the color of the carpet in those offices, it was the most unlikely color any one could imagine. It was white. I asked my boss who was going to clean the carpet. He said that I was. I said you are kidding. He said just do the best I could. I protested with great zeal. He said to just do my regular job and not give the carpet a lot of attention.

In about a month, the beautiful white carpet had turned solid black. Management brought in a cleaning service to steam clean the area. I believe it took the service two days to clean six small offices and a ten foot long hallway. They placed plastic walkways on the floor for people to walk but it did not help because the people that used the offices had to get off the plastic to get to their charts and graphs.

Sometime later, the carpet was removed. It was not a bad idea but the color choice was outrageous. The cost of the debacle I believe was tens of thousands of dollars. I would have chosen a darker color. Management could have used the money constructively. Management had degrees from universities and they claimed to be smarter than I was, but they sometimes showed no common sense. I was just a regular employee but I know white carpet does not go into offices next to the plant floor. A fourth grader could have told them that this particular color scheme was not going to work.

Another example occurred when the company decided to update the packing plant. They brought in robotics to eliminate man power. Great idea in theory I thought. The machines were hurriedly assembled. The machines malfunctioned all the time. They hired two hundred new employees that worked faster than the machines. The machines were placed in storage until a later date. This also cost a great deal of money. I heard that later on they reinstalled the machines with the problems fixed. I never heard what happen to the employees who were there to replace the machines, I hope they were allowed to stay but I do not know what happened to them. (They were laid-off).

These are a few examples how management proved to the employees how smart they were than us. I am sure that they had good days doing things benefiting the workers and suggestions from employees to improve morale and a better working environment.

They still loved living on Mount Olympus looking down their noses at the people that worked on the floor. As long as the rules were followed, everything was fine, but if something went wrong in their eyes a lighting bolt descended from the mountain that the employee was there by their grace. They knew they were in charge giving them a feeling of invincibility. This book will test that invincibility because management will realize the events are true.

It is not hard to be in management. A college degree, shit for brains and an ounce of stupidity. It does not take much thinking to stab someone in the back while climbing the corporate ladder. It takes balls even the women have them. No matter who gets hurt as long as you advance your career. The funny thing is, at least to me, is when they crash and burn.

CHAPTER FIVE

Stupidvisors

A STUPIDVISOR is a SUPERVISOR that is STUPID. Ernest T. Bass from the *Andy Griffith Show* looked like a genius compared to these women and men.

Management came to a brilliant decision to recruit college graduates such as engineers to come and work for XYZ Battery Company. Once they had arrived and settled into the town, then XYZ would say that they did not have any engineer jobs open right now but they could work as a supervisor until a job was open. I know that some of them declined the offer and took jobs elsewhere but most of them said o.k. Now is when the problems start. A college graduate that has just graduated from school who has studied his ass off for four years, who did not have a social life is thrust onto 50 or more workers with 50 different personalities this is where the conflict begins. They are not prepared to be a psychologist, psychiatrist, nurse or a referee. They are engineers period. XYZ Battery Company practically threw them to the wolves. They had one goal, make production.

The engineer would have to come into a new situation and succeed and then receive a promotion. They usually figured that the employees were working for them. They had a gigantic wake up call waiting. The employees working on the floor had been doing their job for a very long time and did not need an over-educated yahoo trying to tell them how to do the job better. Sometimes the engineer would realize that his people knew what they were doing and let them do their job. Stupidvisors like "Jonah", who use to be in lower management thought they had the people skills to handle any situation. "Jonah" should have stayed where he was working. Everyone would have benefited. They soon received a cold lesson in reality. A person has to face the facts when he is over his head, a college grad did not have any people skills.

When the stupidvisor arrived, we would have a shift meeting. The Stupidvisor was determined to show that he was in charge and that his word was law. The job will be performed his way or you could leave, attempting to put the fear of God into us. This was a very big mistake because he would drive a wedge between the workers and himself. He just created 50 new enemies because everyone thought that he was an asshole. The Stupidvisor did not realize that he was working in a factory that involved machines. These machines were old and broke down often. The Stupidvisor tried to put the blame on the employees. He soon realized that the machines did break down and this was not the employee's fault. He would then think that the mechanic was not working fast enough to eliminate the problem.

I remember one Stupidvisor we called "Crazy Horse", who would stand behind a mechanic and tell him the best possible way to fix the problem. This did nothing but make the matter worse. The mechanic, not only became angry but also slowed to a snail's pace. The mechanic was about to whip "Crazy Horse's" butt. I told him that his presence was not needed that he was slowing the mechanic down also the mechanic knew what he was doing. When the machine was ready, I would page him to let him know that we were running again. He returned to his office. He was one of the lucky engineers, an opening in engineering became available and he went into the position. He is no longer with the company. He found a job closer to his family.

The worst Stupidvisor I ever had the displeasure to be around was a woman from South America. Her name was "Carman". Having been released from rehab and needing to be on third shift to attend meetings, I returned to third shift. "Carman" was my Stupidvisor. She did not like me, not the least little bit. She told management that she did not want me on her shift or at least in her crew. Management told her she did not have a choice. She voiced her opinion that this did not make her happy. She was told tough, to try to discover a way, to work with me. I was not happy myself when I found out who my boss was going to be because she thought I was lazy and I thought she was a bitch. She had her pets and everyone else hated her. I decided that I was going to mess with her mind, what little mind she had. She had no personality. She was serious all the time. I often thought that her face would crack if she smiled. She never smiled in my presence so I guess I will never know.

Our line was working 12 hour shifts testing a new product and I was having a hard time staying awake. Falling asleep at work happened every night, no matter how hard a person tried to remain awake. One night I was returning from the restroom, when I saw her waking one of her pets. I did not think much about this at the time but it would benefit me later. We were working overtime that morning and I dozed off and when I awoke, she was standing there with a mean look on her face. She told me to report to her office Sunday night. I reported to her office and she told me to sit down. She said that I was going to receive a written reprimand. I told her to write me up but that I refused to sign the paper and also that I was going to the office to file a complaint against her for harassment. Her face turned a very pretty shade of red. I told her that if she insisted I was in trouble then her pet would be in trouble too. I said that I saw her wake her earlier that evening and that the both of them were having a good laugh about her falling asleep. This really pissed her off tore up the report and told me to return to work. I said o.k. She was constantly watching me. I thought that this was funny because every time that I got the chance to make her life more difficult, i would. This might have been childish but i was having too good of a time tormenting her. I remember one particular night we were having trouble keeping the boxes traveling up the conveyor belt upright because we were running a different brand of battery and the boxes were smaller. (We made other batteries besides our own, the company did not put our name on the battery) she told me to stay at the conveyor belt and stand boxes upright if they fell over. I said that I would be glad to do as she requested. She asked if I could handle the job. I told her a blind monkey could do the job, I said even you. She said do not move from that spot for any reason. I knew this was not going to happen. I stayed in that spot for about an hour. I decided that I needed a smoke, after the last time she checked on me I left. I did not go straight to the restroom. I took the scenic route. I visited with a few friends and goofed off a little before arriving at the restroom. I took my time, smoking two cigarettes instead of one. I finely returned to my work area when I saw "Carman". She did not have a happy look on her face. She asked me where I had been. I told her that I had gone to relieve myself and she then informed me, I was to remain in my assigned area. I said that if I had not left when I had she would have a messy area to clean. She was so mad that she stormed away. I use to go to her office before the shift started to see if I had done anything wrong the previous night to save a trip later. We continued bickering back and forth until she received a promotion to a day shift position. She kept that job for a while until the position no longer existed. She turned down another Stupidvisor position. She said she did not deserve a demotion. She quit her job. I really miss her. I am kidding; she was a pain in the ass.

The real reason that I call a SUPERVISOR a STUPIDVISOR is only for one reason. These people are STUPID, not because they are uneducated but most of them spoke before they took time to think. The Stupidvisor did not have the knowledge to know what to do in a lot of situations. These people were college kids about 21-24. They had never worked in a factory in their life. Management wanted these people to develop people skills but this idea often did not work the way that management intended. The kids were dumped into an environment of ass-holes, bitches, gossipers, smartasses, religious zealots, the hitler youth and people that just wanted to do their job, then go home.

They were very lucky if temporary employees were not involved. The college kids were trained for a couple of weeks before being left on their own. For the record some of the bosses were pretty good because they took the time to learn the employees habits and determined for themselves that the employees knew what they were doing. They also learned about everyone's personality. These people were the exception. Most of the stupidvisors wanted to further their career no matter who might get in the way or whose feelings were hurt. Some of the stupidvisors looked for other jobs because they knew that they had been screwed. The Stupidvisor who thought that he could change the productivity because of his great mind had tough lessons to learn. Every time a Stupidvisor would try to change how production was being run because he thought his way was better found out the hard way that if something is not broken, do not try to fix it. Production dropped off almost every time. When production dropped, upper management wanted to know why the numbers had dropped. The Stupidvisor would say that he had tried a new idea. He was told that he was there to baby sit and to allow the employees to do their jobs because they (employees) knew how to get the job done with the best possible results. It was all right for them to observe and maybe they could learn something.

I have three Stupidvisors to discuss in length. These three touched my life more than all the other bosses put together.

The first boss is "Saul". He was educated somewhere in Tennessee, I do not know where. He was intelligent and had common sense too. These are qualities lacking in most Stupidvisors. He was fair and he would tell you to your face if your work was sub-standard. He also would offer ideas how to perform your job more efficiently. He would tell you what your job was for the night, then let you go do it. He came around occasionally to bullshit but I think he was making sure you were doing your job. He had a great sense of humor. He would back you up in case of a complaint if he believed that you were telling the truth.

An example of his sense of humor was concerning a woman that everyone referred to as "Same O". The reason I named her that is she looked the same in the front as she did in the back. We worked crossword puzzles while we worked, especially when we were letting a floor dry because if we left the area while the floors were still wet people would walk around the wet floor signs and we would have to mop the floors again. Returning to the story, I was waiting for a floor to dry when "Same O" came to me with a problem with her crossword puzzle. I asked her what was wrong. She said that she could not get the words to fit. I looked at the puzzle and started to laugh. #3 Across, the clue was use to be clay. "Same O" had put mud. I told her that the answer was Ali. She said she did not understand. I told her that Cassius Clay had changed his name to Ali when he had converted and became a Muslim. She asked what was Muslim. I said that it was a religion primarily based in the middle east. She begged me not to say anything to anyone. I said that I was going to tell everyone I came in contact. I told "Saul" during lunch. He laughed so hard I think he broke a rib.

Another time a supervisor needed to enter his boss's office to leave a report. I had just waxed the floor and depending on how heavy the coating, drying times differed. The supervisor insisted that he wanted to put the report in the office. I told him that he would have to wait, besides he had 6 hours before his boss would arrive. He insisted strongly that since he was my superior, he was going to place the report in the office. I quietly said no. He said that he would report me to my boss. I told him that he was in his office and be my guest. He started into the hallway leading to "Saul's" office and I followed close behind him knowing that the office he was trying to get to was down the same hallway. He did not know that I was right behind him and he turned a sharp right hoping to get into the office. I stepped in front of him and told him to return when the floor was completely dry. He said that he was my superior again and if he wanted to enter the office, he would. I said no you will not enter the office until the floor was dry. He said that it sounded like I was threatening him. I said it was not a threat; it was a promise. I also told him I did not care if he was the pope he still could not enter. He went to see "Saul". "Saul" told him the same thing but in a much nicer way. He would have to wait until the floor dried. The supervisor said that I had threatened him with bodily harm. "Saul" came to see me. He asked me if I had done what the man had said. I said yes and the reason behind my statement. "Saul" went to the supervisor and told him that I had a schedule to follow and that "Pete's" job was hard enough that if he was allowed to walk on a freshly waxed floor he would have to mop the floor again and to my boss this would be unacceptable. He hoped that he understood. He said that when the floor was dry that "Pete" would tell him that it was o.k. to enter the office. When the floor was dry, I went to the supervisor and told him it was all right to leave his report, I also apologized for my behavior. The supervisor said that the incident was his fault and we should consider the matter even. I excitedly agreed with him then returned to my duties.

I did not mind working overtime for "Saul" even when he asked me at the last minute. The job was easy money because we had to strip the break room floor. The only hard part was removing all the tables and chairs. This job was fun for me because I was in charge. My crew and I would take all the wax off the floor, let it dry then seal twice and wax twice. When the floor dried, we would return the tables and chairs. This event would take 10 to 12 hours. The boring part was the waiting for the floor to dry after each procedure. The job was tedious but someone had to do it, why not me?

I really hated it when I was bumped (transferred) from my job. This meant that I would no longer be working for "Saul". He was a good boss. I heard that he retired because of the political bullshit that went on all of the time. I sincerely hope he is doing well.

The second supervisor I would like to discuss is "Ted". He is the same person that I mentioned earlier in the book who I had worked with in the janitorial service when I first came to third shift. He had been working there as an employee since he graduated from high school. When he left the janitor service, he worked in the can making area. He then decided to become an inspector, the pay was better and this move gave him a better chance to get into management. I also think the job was easier. Eventually he became a supervisor. He had been a regular employee so he knew all the excuses someone could attempt to use to avoid doing their job.

I need to say that "Ted" and I were good friends, next to Leroy and Wyllie. I taught him how to play golf. We also did some partying too. He was a great guy to be around outside of work. He was hard to work for because he would make me do things twice as good as the other employees who knew we were friends. His explanation to me was that he did not want people to think that i was receiving favoritism. Every time our line was not running, he gave the dirtiest jobs in the plant; whether that was cleaning a machine from top to bottom or painting a machine or the floor.

I did have some perks though. I could express my opinion about our situation, no matter the language I used. He would do the same if we were in his office. A lot of people would ask me to speak to him on their behalf because of our friendship. I told them if they had something to say, they should express whatever opinion they might have because our friendship ended as soon as we passed through the gate. This was not exactly true but they did not need to know it. It was none of their concern.

One night I was pushing batteries onto a moving belt that flowed down to the people who were packing. I knew that the time was nearing for break so I looked at the clock on the wall to see how much time until break. Surprisingly I could not see the clock. I could not see the wall either. I got someone to take my place and went to the restroom. I had been gone for 10 minutes when "Ted" stormed into the restroom and asked me "what the hell" was happening. I calmly lit a cigarette and told him that I could not see anything. He really did not believe me. He held three fingers up and asked me how many were showing. I said I did not know because I could not see his hand or for the record, I could not see him. He left to telephone "Rita" who said to take me home. He said that he could not do this because he was the only boss present. She asked if he knew of anyone that he could call and he said that he did. He phoned "Alice" and explained the problem. She came to XYZ Battery Company to get me and take me home. The next day I found out that the reason I had lost my eyesight. I had diabetes. I believe my sugar level was above 400. I was blind about two weeks then my eyesight returned. The reason I mentioned this is because that during my time away from work; "Ted", "Leroy" and "Roscoe" came to my apartment and took me to play golf. The funny thing was that I beat them.

I had developed an infection on my lower leg while I was performing a job when I bumped my leg into a table. I treated the injury with anti-biotic but the injury did not get better, it slowly got worse. Finally, the pain had reached the point where I could no longer do my job. I sat down upon some steps and told "Ted" I could not go anymore. He asked me why. I told him that I was hurt. I showed him my injury and he almost lost his cookies. He sent me home right then. "Alice" inquired about the reason I was home so early. I told her it was not important, we would discuss it in the morning. I was doctoring my leg when she walked into the room and asked me what I was doing. I said that I was applying medicine to my leg. She insisted that she do it. When she saw the condition of my leg, she freaked. She immediately phoned my diabetic doctor. She told the receptionist that I needed to see the doctor now. The receptionist was rude and said the doctor had a full schedule that day and that I could maybe get an appointment later on in the week. "Alice" told the receptionist that we were coming right now and the doctor needed to know that we were on our way because of the urgency of the visit. When we arrived at the doctor's office, we were sent in to see him. He looked at my leg and told me that I would be going to the hospital. I asked him if I had a choice. He said I did have a choice; I could choose what hospital I wanted to have my surgery. I chose the one that did not smell like a hospital. I was admitted that same afternoon. The doc came by to see me and told me that if I had waited a little longer I could have lost my leg. There was a possibility this still might happen. I said that would not happen because they do not make peg legs with golf spikes. He did not find humor in my comment. I had the surgery and my leg survived. I was in the in the hospital about 3 weeks. "Ted" visited once. I think that "Leroy" made him do this though I cannot prove that this occurred. This upset me deeply. I believe he stayed about 15 minutes. He visited soon after my surgery and I was stoned out of my mind, so I barely remember the visit.

"Ted" was all right to work with even though I strongly recommend that unless you have to work with a friend do not. He divorced his wife and is dating a woman named "Lassie". The last time I saw him he was doing fine. He was fired from XYZ Battery Company. Stupidvisors employed with the company have certain perks. Longevity is not one of the perks. One day you can be doing a perfect job and the next day, you can lose that job. This is what happened to "Ted". He reported to work on Monday and was informed that his services were no longer needed. I believe this had something to do with him living with "Lassie" but I am not sure. This is my opinion. I do know that XYZ Battery Company lost a great supervisor that day. Management really screwed themselves with that decision.

The third Stupidvisor that I would like to discuss is the Stupidvisor of all Stupidvisors. If you looked up the word Stupidvisor in the dictionary, you would find her picture. There is nothing that I can say good about this woman, so I won't. She once said to me that she was not there to make friends, good thing because she did not have many. I would trust Osama Bin Laden before her. Dealing with Osama Bin Laden at least a person knows what to expect. "Jezebel" had so many faces and personalities, a person never knew which personality to expect. I tried my very best to avoid her. She was the stupidvisor who was in charge of the powder room on third shift at the battery making plant. I do not believe that I ever saw her clean. I worked for her one day but I could not do the job that she wanted me to perform. The job was too high and I would have to walk on a narrow ledge, so I refused to do that job.

An example of "Jezebel's" deadpan personality and great scheming ability was that she had no feelings. She had her own nephew fired for doing something that she told him to do in the first place. "Wylie", was an inspector in her area. His job was to make sure the powder mixture and the size of the cans were the right size. If there was a problem he was suppose to put that particular batch on hold. This meant that the product would be put to the side and more tests would have to be performed on the cans before they would be either scrapped or placed into production. "Wylie" went to his aunt and informed her of the problem. She asked him to recheck the cans and he said that he had all ready checked it twice. He said that he had no choice but to put the batch on hold. She asked him to let the batch go and if there was a problem she would have his back. I know that this is true because i was in the break room cleaning the cafeteria. He made the mistake by trusting her. The mistake was later discovered by another inspector. "Wylie" was summoned before management to explain why he did not put the batch on hold or at least report the problem to the stupidvisor. He said that he had told "Jezebel" and that she said to go ahead and let the batch through. Management called her into the office and asked her why she had not stopped production to fix the problem. She informed management she had not been told of any problem because if she had she would have shut down the machines to have them fixed. She was a stupidvisor and "Wylie" being only an inspector, one can guess whose story that management believed. Yes, they believed her.

This happened on a Friday and we were having our annual golf outing that afternoon, a decision would be made the following Monday. A team, which consisted of management who were investigating the incident, were playing in the outing and had all ready, made up their minds. The management team being "drunker than football bats" informed "Wylie" that he was fired.

I am no genius but that is no way to fire someone. It proved to me that management had no class whatsoever. I thought that the way that management had acted was shitty and I was going to say something to them but "Saul" advised me not to say anything.

Looking back this was the best thing that could happen to "Wylie". He returned to the service where he remains today.

The following Monday I went to "Jezebel", being pissed off I asked her why she had stabbed her own flesh and blood in the back, especially since she had told him that she would stand behind him if a problem arose. She said that she had thought that management was going to make someone the scapegoat. She said if someone was to get into trouble that she was not going to be that person. She said that she had no choice but to lie. I told her that I should go up front and tell management the truth since I had heard the entire conversation. She did not believe me she thought "Wylie" had told me. I informed her that I was in the room when she said to him that she would have his back in case of trouble. I told her that "Wylie" had asked me not to say anything to management but I told her to stay the hell away from me because I knew enough about her that she would be next to go.

These are just three examples of the kind of supervisors and stupidvisors we had at XYZ Battery Company. A few were very good at their job, well liked by their crews but most were

exceptionally Stupid in their own unique way.

CHAPTER SIX

Employees

There are three very different kinds of people that work at XYZ Battery Company. Luckily, they all work on different shifts. Each shift has their own characters that if they worked on another shift would go completely nuts. The shifts were as different as night and day. Each shift had a diverse personality and if a person did not fit into that shift's personality, he or she should move onto another shift or maybe change plants.

The FIRST SHIFT was a menagerie of old timers, ass kissers, stupidvisor's pets and people that would do anything to move up the company ladder. I know I have discussed some employees before but I will talk about them at great detail in this chapter.

The people who worked on day shift were mostly women. I really do not believe that they were there to work. I believe they showed up to style and profile. We use to stand at the time clock waiting to go home when the first shift people who were running a bit late would walk by and we would nearly be knocked out by the whiff of their perfume. First shift was more like a beauty pageant rather than a work place.

There were also the squealers who would tell on their own families if they thought it would get them special favors from their boss. I tried to avoid these people no matter how much they wanted to be friends.

Then there were the gossipers, who with just a touch of fact would make up the rest in order to get ahead or get someone into trouble. They were also trying to get into their bosses good graces. I avoided these people too.

It was very rare that I would find a person that was friendly, hard working and normal. The people were content on doing their jobs but I did locate a few. I was very fortunate to work with these ladies during my first three months. They were some of the finest people I have ever had the pleasure to work with and be around. I would have done anything for them.

The mechanics and inspectors were good people; they performed their jobs without complaint and at their own convenience. They took no crap from anyone. I liked and respected all of them. I believed that they should have been in charge and recalling my recollections I think that they were in charge.

The company had employed the people that worked on first shift for a very long time. Most of them were arrogant and set in their ways. If they took the time to give you advice, they expected you to follow that advice. They considered themselves smarter than a supervisor, since supervisors often changed, I did not follow their advice but I did listen. The advice came in handy in the future. I learned that I should listen to anyone who had something interesting to say. When I was hired and placed on first shift, I really wanted to remain on first shift. I now am glad that I was moved. I did not fit in with the people. The people on first shift were set in their ways. I was too easy going to have to work with these people. I had too much fun doing my job. First shift was too up-tight for me. I was not a snitch, back stabber or an old person trying to look pretty. I just wanted to work my forty and go home. I was not looking for trouble and did not want to cause any problem. I wanted to make friends that saw the world the same way as i did and have fun along the way, while doing our job. These people did not exist on first shift.

The people that worked on SECOND SHIFT either were married or did not have a life other than work. The younger employees did not like to be there because all a person could do on this shift was to work, sleep and eat, except on weekends unless a person had to work on the weekend then the weekend was ruined. Second shift was the best shift for married employees because there was no time to spend money except on the family.

The people on this shift wanted to be there or they were being punished. The time I spent on second shift I felt isolated from the rest of the world. Very few people liked second shift. The married people did not mind it as much because it gave them a break from their older children and allowed them more time with their younger ones. I lived in another city about 40 miles away, so I got to my favorite bar a little after midnight to have a nightcap before going home.

Second shift also had its religious zealots. They always wanted to give me their testimony, which I really did not want to hear. I do believe in God. I do not think work is the place for this activity.

I usually did not believe the way they did, so I would decline their offer. This action would only make them try harder. I would finally let them do want they had intended to do and then they would ask me if I wanted to attend church with them on Sunday. I would graciously decline and tell them that I had other plans. I was going to play golf but they did not need to know what my intentions were. They had achieved their goal and I had not hurt their feelings. I do believe that I am a Christian but I think that the entire world is the church and I do not think a person has to be in a building to worship God as some so-call Christians do one day a week.

Second shift had their own snitches and back stabbers too. There were not as many as day shift but there were quite a few. These people wanted day shift plain and simple. Day shift had too many chiefs and not enough indians. An example would be that a boss would give you a job to do, then another boss would come by and take you off that job to do something else. The first boss would see you away from the job that he had you doing in the first place and rush over to ask you what you were doing. I would say that another boss had told me to do this job. The boss would then inquire which boss had moved me. I would point him out to my boss and he would go and ask the other boss why he had moved me in the first place. He also told him that I did not work for him anyway. My boss would then tell me to return to my original place, which I did. This sounds confusing I know but that is how things worked at XYZ Battery Company almost every day. I did not want any part of day shift.

I did not fit in on second shift; I did not make many friends. I wanted to do my job and leave. The only job that I enjoyed was when I worked in the laundry room.

In the laundry room, I was my own boss. I had a boss but I only saw him on payday. I had to wash and dry the clothes then fold them neatly and put them in the correct baskets. Sometimes just for fun I would put a large uniform in a smaller person's basket to see or hear the reaction the following day. I also had to clean the men's and women's shower area making sure they had a sterile environment. The only job that I really hated was when I had to foam the shower areas. The men's was not so bad because it was one big shower but for some reason the women had a stall each. This job was a real pain in the ass.

My job was timing, hurry up and wait. The washers and dryers were on timers so I could perform my other duties before the clothes were clean. I would clean the women's first then the first load would be done and I would put that load in the dryers. I would then put the second load in the washers and put the first load in the dryers. Next, I would clean the men's shower and restroom. The dryers would be finished running and I would start folding clothes to put into the baskets.

I did have a few perks, though. I listened to a radio and I brought in food and drink in a cooler. When my work was finished, I sometimes took a nap. I liked the job even if the job was on second shift.

I did clash with another stupidvisor once. I guess I was not doing my job to his satisfaction. He called me into the office for a discussion. He cussed me like a drunken sailor that had just returned from leave, after he had been at sea for 6 months. I told him to kiss my ass. He said he was going to have me fired. I said go ahead and try. He said to come in early tomorrow. I asked if I was going to be paid for coming in early. He said no. I said that I would see him at the regular time. He changed his mind and told me to clock in an hour early. The lady on day shift was shocked to see me when I got there the next day. I explained to her that I had a meeting, which I had to attend. I went into the ass-hole's office and his boss was waiting to talk to me. I said hello to his boss and asked him how he was doing, he said fine. The stupidvisor was surprised to see that I knew him. He informed his boss that I had told him to kiss his ass. His boss asked me if I had said those words to the stupidvisor. I said that I had but that he had cussed me first. He asked me what the stupidvisor had said. I said that he stated that I was a cripple asshole who had no fucking business working for the company and if he had his way, he was going to give my fucking job to a normal person. He asked my boss if he had used those exact words. The dumbass admitted to saying those words. I was told by his boss to return to my job. I was not in trouble. When I left the office, I could hear his boss yelling at the stupidvisor for being an insensitive ass. I think the whole area heard him even with the door closed. His boss came back to see me after he had finished screaming at the stupidvisor. He told me that I had made one mistake. I had cussed him too. He said that if I had taken his verbal abuse and then filed a complaint he would have been looking for new employment. I said that I had learned a valuable lesson and that I was grateful that he listened to both sides of the story. He did say that he did not like my boss either and would love to get rid of him but he has too many friends in the front office.

The most fun I ever had was working on THIRD SHIFT or as my dad called it, GRAVE YARD. Third shift had the most interesting people, at both plants. The people on third shift were considered the outcasts of the company. The pot heads, pill poppers, smartasses, assholes, hard heads and the funniest people i have ever had the pleasure to meet.

The best stupidvisors were on third shift, mainly because of the number. There was two maybe, mostly just one at the packing plant. The stupidvisors on third shift were more relaxed because

Their boss was not looking over his/her shoulder. They knew their workers on a first name basis along with their abilities. There was only one bad boss on third shift at each plant but I have all ready mention them, so I will not repeat myself. I wish to discuss the employees in this chapter.

Third shift was where I met my friends and they still are my friends today. I will discuss my friends later. I want to discuss the people that I met that were acquaintances.

"Amos" was the first person whom I worked with at the packing plant in the janitorial service. I learned a lot of lessons about life from him. I learned never take anything for granted. Expect the unexpected. Try to get away with as much as you can without drawing suspicion to yourself. Do not; I repeat take no shit from anyone. If you do, people will try to boss you around. Be a man and stand behind your work. Make sure your work is done right then you can do whatever you want to do. Stay away from the boss because if he thinks you have extra time he will find more work for you. Do not act intelligent because if management discovers that you are smart then they will expect more from you; act dumb and they will leave you alone. I wish now looking back that I had acted as smart as I really am because I believe this would have benefited in the end. However, I wanted to keep my personal life and my work life completely different, something like the difference between church and state. This action hurt me later on during my career when I applied for a job as an inspector. Management did not think that I was smart enough to do the job. I did make the short list and was granted an interview. I thought it was funny that management considered me dumb and stupid. I knew that I was just as smart as most of them, a college degree does not make you intelligent, at XYZ Battery Company it only made you a smartass. "Amos" and I always had some time to catch a nap before the morning rush. We had separate jobs to do but we discovered that if we did our jobs together that we could do them twice as fast and were done quicker. We did our jobs in 4 hours instead of eight. This gave us time to take a nap. "Amos" disappointed me when he said that we were not friends but were acquaintances. This upset me greatly. I told "Leroy" and he said do not let the idiot's comment bother me because he was full of himself. Still, I thought that I had made a new friend because good friends are hard to attain. I was glad when he quit the company after we were bumped from our jobs. I think management was happy too. I thought that he was stupid for quitting his job after being on the job for 10 years and he did not have another job to go to yet. I tried to talk to him about his decision but he had already made up his mind. He said the company would miss him after he was gone but no one even noticed. I think his girlfriend missed him but nobody else did. He was my favorite acquaintance. I missed him for a little while but I got over those thoughts quickly.

The use of drugs and smoking pot was done often from the mid eighties to the early nineties at the company on all three shifts. I thought that the employees considered it a sport or a hobby. The employees took every drug, legal or illegal that a person could imagine. The police could have tested my entire shift and everyone including myself would have tested positive. I use to go to my car and have a few drams of whiskey. During the winter, six of us would go to an employees car and smoke a joint during break. When the company implemented a drug policy most of the employees stopped using drugs before, during and after work because we did not want to lose our jobs. One gentleman did not stop. A person could set his/her watch by him going to his car at break to smoke some pot. This idiot would always park his car under a parking lot light so he could see. It took the company a while before they discovered that he was using drugs all the time. I think they even put him in rehab. However, this did not help and he was eventually dismissed. The company never conducted a random drug test unless a person had an accident on a tow motor. I think it was added to the rules to scare us. It served its purpose. I have to give management credit; I did not think that they were that smart or maybe they got some information from a snitch.

A person needed to have an attitude before you started working on third shift. If you did not have one you had two choices; bid off third shift or develop one.

You needed to get along with the people who worked in your area, this made the night goes by much faster and it was fun. The night that the braves beat the pirates to advance to the world series, we were listening to the game on the radio. The entire line was excited that the braves had won. The stupidvisor came by the line to tell us that the braves had won the game and we had to act as if we did not know the outcome. After he had left all of us laughed. We saw our boss maybe once a night unless we were having mechanical problems. He would come by twice on Friday; once to tell us what we were running and the other time to give us our paychecks.

We knew what we were doing anyway so the stupidvisor did not bother to come to our line unless he had too. He did not want to hear some of the topics we discussed; from sex to sports. We really did not discuss sex very often because the line liked to keep our personal lives separate. We only discussed sex if a person had a problem and wanted a solution. We listened to her dilemma and then offered her several suggestions how to fix the problem. She listened to our suggestions and acted accordingly. This usually worked.

The main topic we discussed, at least on our line was some stupid new regulation that was going to be added to the rules. An example would be that smoking cigarettes was banned inside the plant. Those of us that smoked had to go outside during breaks and lunch to smoke. We felt that this was unfair because it is very cold in the winter at night. We asked them if there was somewhere, we could smoke inside without bothering the other employees. We were told definitely not. We were told if we did not like the new rule, we could always quit smoking for health reasons. We nixed that idea mainly because we enjoyed smoking and it made management unhappy. During the winter, we stood in the doorway to block the wind so we would not get sick. During the spring, summer and fall we just went outside. We were often late returning to our positions on the line but we just told our boss that we did not change the rules, they did.

We broke the rules every chance we had the opportunity. Someone could call it the nature of the beast I guess. The more rules that management added to the books, the more ways we tried to get around them and get away with technicalities. I always felt that I was working for big brother like the people in "George Orwell's" book 1984.

My favorite people on third shift besides my closest friends were the mechanics. They were the coolest people I had met since the bikers that I use to hang around with in Nashville. If they like a stupidvisor, they did their best to get a machine running as fast as they could. If they did not like the stupidvisor, they would take forever to do the job. They did not take any shit from anyone. Gaining their trust was hard but if you were able to do this and became their friend, even if they did not like the boss, they would fix your machine as fast as they could. The mechanics were a great bunch of guys. If you showed interest, they would show you how to fix a minor problem without having to call for a mechanic. This would save time also it would allow the mechanics to be doing other things that had to be done before the next shift arrived.

There were two women that no matter how hard I tried I could not get along. The first girl was a black woman but that was not the reason we did not see eye to eye. She was fucking nuts! An example would be that she sent herself flowers on her birthday and on valentine's day. She was always trying to get me in trouble. One particular night, she told me to get my gd ass back to our machine. I was trying to help another person that was new to the job, teaching her how to fix her machine. I told her to fuck off. She went straight to the stupidvisor and informed him that I had cussed her. He came over to where I was and took me into the office. He asked me if I had cussed her, which I answered yes. He asked me why I had done such a thing. I told him that she had cussed me first and that I was helping the person who was new to the job. He asked me what she said. I told him exactly what she said word for word. He told me to return to my job and if the new girl needed any more help, help her. He took the girl into the office who had complained in the first place and asked her why she did not tell the entire story. She said that she had not said anything but when the other people on the line were interviewed, they agreed with me. The woman had a bad report placed in her file and she left me alone for the duration of her time at XYZ Battery Company. She was dismissed for reasons I cannot recall but I was glad when I found out that she no longer worked there.

The other girl that was employed there who I will refer to as "Lassie" because she reminds me of a dog. She is a loud mouth cussing broad who kissed the ass of every boss she ever worked for and basically got away with murder. She especially kissed my friend Ted's butt and the idiot bought this hook line and sinker. She made her share of mistakes but the mistakes were always someone else's fault. One time the strips that we used to test the batteries were missing from the package. My operator was supposed to be watching my part of the line while I was in the restroom. I think I was away from the machine three minutes tops. The operator was down on her end of the line talking to the mechanic. The strips were missing from the packs. I shut the machine down to retrieve the bad packs. "Lassie" worked on the machine that packaged the boxes into larger boxes to be shipped. I told her she had to shut down her line, in order for me to find the bad packs of batteries. She went ballistic. She always bitched if she had to get her fat ass out of her chair and do some work. I had retrieved all the packs without strips, when she decided to inform, "Ted" that I was not doing my job. He asked me what my problem was and I told him I had to take a leak. I also told him that it did not hurt her to have to work occasionally and that he might keep her "fat free ass" off my back.

Sadly, "Ted" and "Lassie" are living together now. I feel sorry for "Ted" but he seems to like her a lot. He divorced a real pain in the ass and now he lives with another. I think that those types of women are the type he feels comfortable being in his life. Someday I hope someone comes along that he might love and have a personality that is good for him but as of right now life goes on.

One night "Alice" (my wife) and the rest of the people that worked on her line were having a hard time staying awake, especially hard when a person has to stand all the time. Management finally realized that these people could do their work better if they were sitting in a chair but I guess it takes brilliant minds longer to think of things that make common sense. The employees came up with an idea, which was to sing. They began to sing "joy to the world", not the Christmas song but the rock song. Everyone started singing until they got to the first line of the first verse, which was Jeremiah, was a bullfrog. The lady who had taken me to the office for swearing at her became hysterical because her husband's name was Jeremiah. She threatens to kick my wife's ass. "Alice" tried to explain to her that it is the words to the song that it does not refer to her husband in any way. The woman shut her mouth without speaking another word. The rest of the line continued singing for the duration of the night. "Alice" told me about the incident when the shift was over. I thought it was funny and I told her not to worry about her because she was fucking nuts!

There was another time when a guy who I thought was my friend, told another friend that I was in love with her. I guess it did not dawn on him that she was gay or that I was happily married at the time. I did not find out this information until the following day when "Ted" told me at the golf course. I was livid. He said that the girl wanted either her, or me transferred I said I did not say anything even close to that remark. I told him that I would straighten things out Sunday night. He said that I had better do just that very thing. I went to work on Sunday, cornering my "friend" asking him what the hell he was trying to do. I said he really screwed up this time. I asked him what possessed him to tell her something like that anyway. He said that I had given her a teddy bear. I told the stupid idiot that the reason I gave her the teddy bear was that she was going into the hospital, it would give her a buddy so she would not ever be alone. I told him that he needed to go tell her that he had been mistaken or I would kick the shit out of him. He went over to her and said that what he had said before was wrong and hoped she would accept his apology. She was furious. She told him in no uncertain terms that he almost ruined a good friendship because he did not know any of the facts. I told him that I would never trust him again mainly because he spoke without thinking. He said that he was sorry and that he would be more careful in the future. He no longer works for the company; it seems that while he was on medical leave he forgot that when he returned to work the company gives you a blood test. He had smoked some "dope" prior to returning and failed the test. He was fired.

During my second year of employment just before Christmas shutdown, the workers were in a partying mood. I was on janitor duty, which includes taking out the trash. On that night, I must have made about twenty trips to the dumpster. I had mixed together some refreshment like Bourbon and Coke, Bourbon and Sprite along with a batch of Screwdrivers in 2 liter bottles so that anyone could have a drink free. I hid the bottles under the garbage. I did not have any trouble getting rid of the refreshment before management reported for work. I think that everyone took a drink, some even took more than that but everyone seemed glad that I had thought of doing this for my fellow workers. I really feel that I made new friends that night. I got rid of the empty bottles in the trash compactor without any problem.

Everyone was doing something that night. They were drinking or smoking marijuana. One guy had hid a bottle of Bourbon on the back dock. His boss smelled alcohol on his breath and asked him where he had hid the bottle. The boss told his employee that if he told him where he had hid the bottle, he would make sure that he was called back to work after shutdown. I felt sorry for the guy because I knew the boss was lying, he just wanted the liquor for himself. The guy said that the liquor was on the back dock behind some broken pallets. The boss went to the dock to retrieve the alcohol but it was not there. The guy told his boss that was where he placed the bottle and showed him exactly where he had hid it. The bottle was missing. I do not believe the boss bought his story. The bottle had been exactly where the guy said he placed it but I saw him put it there and I took the bottle and put it in my car. The guy wasn't recalled to work and he moved back to Florida.

A woman who also worked at XYZ Battery Company was constantly horny. She had sex with a number of men who worked there too. She was so easy that she got the nickname "Deep and Wide". During lunch breaks, she and boyfriend of the month would go out to the parking lot, to have sex. They did not know they were being watched or they did know and did not care. I guess a person had seen the act in progress to think it was funny, but it was funny to see the van bouncing up and down. All good things end though. They were told on by snitches and were caught in the act and fired.

"Chloe", was trying to fill a pallet of batteries before shift change 1 night, when the pallet broke and batteries went all over the place. Third shift had to fill the pallet or day shift would receive credit for the pallet even if they only completed one layer. When the pallet broke, I busted into laughter. I was going to help her pick up the batteries but I could not stop laughing. "Chloe" got pissed off and told me to go away. I was smoking a cigarette, when my boss walked towards me and asked me why I was not helping her pick up the batteries from the floor. I told him that I had offered but since I had laughed, she said that she did not want or need my help. He said to help her anyway which I did still chuckling to myself. She is my friend but every time I think about the incident, I still am tickled.

When I was working in the janitorial service, we would work two shifts one after the other. The first shift we would strip a floor and then do our regular job the next shift. This was easy at first when I was young but as I got older, I decided working six days a week was better. I did not get as tired and I was primarily in charge. I had to make sure the job was done correctly and quickly.

The people that worked third shift liked me or hated me, no in between. I was not a fence sitter. The people that did not like me thought I was faking my handicap to get easier jobs. I was watched constantly to make sure that I limped all the time or that I did something with my right hand. I was asked more than once by management if I was cured of my handicap. I tried to explain that my CP was a birth defect and no cure existed. This accusation made me angry the first few times the question was brought to my attention, after that I would just turn and walk away, thinking how these people got through college with brains that small. I did not take any shit from anyone. This one particular woman told me she knew that I was faking my handicap and I proceeded to tell her to "eat me". "Leroy" said that I had better be careful to whom I said anything towards but I said that I was tired of their idiotic statements, and I was not going to take their crap any longer.

The type of person I most despise is a former smoker. I do not blame anyone for stopping; what I do not like is anyone telling me all frigging day that smoking was a bad habit. This person continued for a year or more when one day he caught me in a bad mood. I told this man that if he said another word to me about the evils of smoking that I was going to shove a lit cigarette so far up his ass that smoke would come out of his ears. He quit preaching or even talking to me and that made me very happy.

I had a black friend whom I will refer to as "Stew". He first job was an inspector then moved into the chemical lab. We did not get along at first because he was sensitive. He was angry with black people not receiving the recognition as quickly as they should. He had a valid point. I knew how he felt; I thought it would be fun to tease him about his attitude. When I was the janitor, I cleaned the lab. One night he was saying that it was time that the blacks received their reward for quality work. I told him not to worry about it. He asked why he should not be concerned. I told him that he was brown not black. I must admit that this statement was not the best thing to say but I did make the stupid statement and I will stand by what I said. It was definitely wrong. This made him very angry. I told him that I was joking and that I agreed with his remarks. I asked him if he felt so strongly, why not do something about the situation. He said that he could lose his job if he said anything but that he thought that things would get better in the future. When I got ahead in my work, I would stop by the lab for a chat. "Stew" was a very intelligent man and had a great personality. He had plans for life after XYZ Battery Company. He had a very good-looking wife and a son. We would sit around and find amusement with the daily rumor mill at the plant. When there were no rumors circulating, we would start a rumor to see how fast it would spread throughout the plant and then laugh our butts off.

"Stew" did tell me a story that concerned the time he was in high school. A teacher that he detested was retiring and he brought a cake from home for her going away party. He told the other students not to eat any of the cake because he had made it just for her. They agreed with some despair. He did not tell anyone that the icing on the cake was nothing but ex-lax. He heard later that she was sick for several days. We got a good laugh about the story. We became great friends even though I have lost touch with him. I heard he almost lost his job about a mistake that he supposedly made in the lab. Management blamed him because he was outspoken. They moved him to second shift, thinking this would make him quit. He went to second shift because he had a family to care for and he was not going to let them run him off his job. I hope he achieved the goals that he wanted and I hope he is doing well.

We actually had a mechanic I did not like. He was a complete dumbass. He claimed to be a man of god, as "Jim Jones" was a man of god. We did not get along. The very first time we met he referred to me as a heathen. I allowed this slight dig to pass because I told him that he did not know me and he should take the time to do just that very thing. The next time that we had a disagreement he called me a "CGDMFSOB". (The first letter stands for cripple, the rest of the initials you can figure out for yourself). I was furious and I wanted to kick his ass. My boss talked me out of doing this saying I would most likely be fired. He was trying to provoke me and I should pay no attention to him. Luckily I was transferred to the other plant the next week. He was transferred there about 6 months later on a different shift. He lost his job about three years later for harassing another employee. She was not the person that turned him in to management. It was another woman sitting next to her. She did not like him talking in the manner, which he was talking. She said that his language was offensive. This particular incident was not the only reason that he was fired, his mechanical skills sucked. I did not feel sorry for him or miss him; he deserved what he got though I did learn a good lesson from his dismissal. A person has to be careful what they say to another person and remember who is working around them because it could cost them their job.

The next employee that I want to mention is "Hans". He is the most obnoxious person I have ever had the displeasure to meet. He was born in Europe and moved to the northeast at an early age. I would run into him from time to time not by choice but because he worked with "Leroy". He had an opinion about everything and his opinion was always right unless you could provide evidence saying he was mistaken. He had started working for XYZ Battery Company in the late eighties. I have never hated a person that quickly except for that stupid mechanic who I already mentioned. It usually takes me awhile, at least for me to like someone or not. Regarding "Hans", I did not like him right away. I cannot think of anything good to say about him so I want try. I just thought that I would mention him in the book, even though he will be mentioned in the next chapter. I always thought he would have made a great Stupidvisor.

I now would like to discuss a friend named "Herman". He introduced me to my present wife. He was so paranoid. He did not trust very many people. We worked together off and on until he transferred to the dirty plant. He was funny, very funny. He was smart in many ways. One misgiving that he had; he liked to smoke pot. This event happened often after the company came out with the new drug policy. "Herman", "June" and I went to his supplier to pick up a bag. After scoring the bag, we drove around for an hour because "Herman" thought the police were following us. Convinced that we were not being followed we returned to my motel room and proceeded to get messed up. We had a falling out in 1993, when my wife and I had a party at our apartment. This party was supposed to be a small gathering of friends from work. The party however got out of hand. Some idiot brought cocaine and I got very mad. I told them that they had to leave because I did not consider going to jail an option I wanted to consider. They got nasty and said they were going to leave and travel to the big city. I said be my guest and have a wonderful time. Meanwhile, I wondered where my wife had disappeared to with "Herman". I started to look in the bedroom, when they opened the door. My wife was upset and "Herman" was stoned. I asked her what was wrong and she said she would tell me later. "Herman" did not say anything and left with the others. When everyone had gone, my wife told me that "Herman" had behaved badly. She said that the entire thing had begun innocently. He had asked her if she would like to smoke a joint. She said that she would enjoy getting high.

They proceeded to go into the bedroom so they would not have to share with anyone else. When he thought she was stoned, he made advances towards her in a sexual nature. She told him no. He still moved forward when my dog started growling at him, getting ready to bite him. He then backed off. It was a good thing that he left when he did or I would have beaten him with a golf club whether he was stoned or sober. The fact that he had left gave me time to think about the incident and plan my next move. I went to work the next working day and told him that my wife had told me what he had attempted to do to my her. He really was scared and asked me what I intended to do about the matter. I said that I was not going to do anything, he was. He asked me what he could do to correct the situation. I said after work he was going to come to my house and apologize to my wife. He asked if this was his only way out of this mess. I said no, I could beat him over the head with a golf club. He opted for choice number 1. He then asked if she would still be asleep. I said no, that she would be awake because I told her that you would be coming by to see her. He really was not up to it but apologized anyway. We did not see him very much after this but I heard he married a 15 year old girl and had a child then divorced, with him gaining custody of the child. I believe he still works for XYZ Battery Company. I hope he is doing fine.

Just after I broke up with my girlfriend, who was married I began hanging around with a woman named "June". We had only one thing in common; we both liked to drink. We worked second shift together and when we got off for the night, I would go buy a case of beer. I also carried a bottle of bourbon in my golf bag and we would take a shot of bourbon, then chase it with beer. We would do this activity until dawn or passed out, which ever came first. Sometimes we would have other friends over for the night but most of the time it was just her and I. We did not date officially, we never had sex we just liked to party. Frankly, she was too strange. Her mood could and did often change in a New York minute. We had some good times and bad times, mostly bad. I discovered that she was using cocaine I told her that I would not be seeing her anymore. Drinking was all right to me but cocaine was illegal and I would not or could not be around someone who used drugs. The funny part of this part of the story is that I now use prescription drugs a great deal stronger than almost anything I could buy on the street. We stayed friends until she lost her job because of attendance problems even though she did return as a temporary worker. When she did return she had quit using drugs and become a decent person. She had a couple of great children. I figured she had to straighten herself up or lose custody of them.

I had the honor of working with a lot of great people. I was requested by someone in management to spy on my fellow employees to find out if anyone were breaking the rules. I told him there was no way in hell that I would inform on another employee, no matter if I liked him or not. They had enough snitches working there to get dirt on someone. I did not care if my job depended on me being an informant, I would not spy for him. The majority of the people who worked at XYZ Battery Company were good honest people. They gave a hard days work for a decent wage. There was twice as many good people than there were bad people. I do not remember all of their names unless I happen to see them in person. Those people I wish well and a good life. Those that I have mentioned in this chapter, with very few exceptions can kiss my southern ass!

CHAPTER SEVEN

Work And Golf

I began playing golf when I was twelve years old. I had played baseball and basketball until then but I quit playing those sports because I was not good enough. My dad's boss had given me a set of right-handed clubs but I was not very good from the right side because of my disability. I got my first set of left-handed clubs soon after my dad figured out I could play better from that side. I could not hit the ball very far, so I practiced my chipping and I would spend hours on the putting green. Dad always told me a good short game would benefit me one day. I remember going to the golf course with the other boys in my neighborhood and play from dawn to dusk. We would play until we ran out of balls, then go find some in the woods and the creek then play some more. It only cost two dollars to play all day and we got our money's worth. I could not hit the ball as far as everyone else but I did have a better short game than the rest of the guys so I usually beat them. I had finally found a sport that I could play and not feel embarrassed. The older I got the better I got. I even made the high school team, where the highlight of my high school golfing career was that I beat a guy who later pitched in the pros. He could hit the ball a long ways but did not have a short game. I beat him quiet easily. I also played on my junior college team. I did not hit the ball very far but I did hit the ball straight and I still had a good short game.

Three friends and I would play every Saturday early in the morning where our parents belonged. We had to play in the morning before the members played in their matches because we were not old enough to play with them yet. A person had to be 18 before he could play in those matches. We had some exciting matches and lots of fun.

When we turned 18, we were allowed to play with the older men. The first time I played my dad wanted me to meet and play with some of the other members so he did not choose me to be on his team. He and I always had an agreement that if one of us won money, the person who won money would return his low-ball money to the other. My first low-ball no one chose me until the next to the last pick. The choices were between a nice eighty-year-old man and me. My captain said that I had to be better than mister "butters" was and asked me if I rode a cart. I said yes sir I did. He chose me. As they were leaving the choosing room, dad told my captain that he had made the right choice. I think I shot 76 and had five birdies. We won the low-ball. My captain told me that he would choose me sooner next time. I smiled and said that would be great.

Through a lot of time and effort, I finally became the number one captain in the low-ball. My handicap was three. I did not stay number one very long but I did shoot in the seventies consistently.

The golf club had and still has a great deal of good people for members. I will never forget one particular select-shot outing that we had. We played select-shot every Friday. (Select-shot is when the entire team tees off from the tee and then the team captain decides which ball would be the best for the rest of the team through the end of the hole) i was late so someone else picked my team. They chose for me three long hitters that did not know where the ball was going and a blind guy. We teed off last and while we were waiting our turn, someone said that my team did not have a snowball chance in hell to win. I smiled and said anything could happen. I told my team that as long as we do not give up that we had a chance to win. My team played the first nine holes five under par. I was told in the clubhouse that one team was seven under. I told my team that we still had a chance. We played the next nine holes ten under par to finish fifteen under par and we won by two shots. We won $110.00 A piece and we had a good time.

I almost became an assistant pro at a private club in upper east Tennessee but the pro decided to marry and took a job with a salvage company. I almost got my dream job but some things do not always turn out like we would hope.

My favorite tournament was when we played the course backwards. There would be four man teams or three men and a woman. An example would be the team would tee off from the back or side of the first green and play to the eighteenth green until the teams had played the entire course. This event was exciting to say the least. The winning scores were not as low but the event was fun. Most of my time at this golf club was an enjoyable experience in my life. I miss the members living and those who have passed. I played there for ten years and I will never forget the memories, some good and some bad.

I use to go to a public course after my divorce looking for a game. I would be practicing on the practice green when I would notice some men watching me practice putting. I would start missing putts on purpose. One of the men would come over to me and ask if I would like to play nine holes with he and his friends. They said that betting was involved, would that be a problem. I would say no if it was not too much money. He would say five dollars a hole and I said fine. I checked my wallet to see how much money I would have left after paying for green fee and a cart. I had fifty dollars and I figured that would be enough. I would limp down to the tee, draging my clubs behind me. I would look at them and they would be smiling. I believe I shot a thirty-four and won about two hundred dollars. I still remember them cussing me as they were paying their debt. I politely said that they had asked me to play because they thought they could take advantage of me. Those remarks silenced them very quickly.

When I first started to work at XYZ Battery Company, I did not know if anyone played golf. I was on day shift during my first few months and the only person that knew I played was the personnel manager. He did not know how good I was, or if I played terribly. The plant manager approached me to ask me if I would like to play in the company's annual golf outing. I told him that I would like that very much and I thanked him for asking me. He said that the event would be held at the local country club. He also said I could leave work early, saying I would receive a complete day's pay. I thought to myself how cool. He also said that there would be an open bar and a steak dinner after the outing. He asked me if I had my golf clubs with me. I said wherever I go they go too. I felt like a child in a candy store when he said that there would be an open bar. An example would be telling a family of big eaters that they could eat as much food as they wanted because it was free. I left work when I was told that I could leave and went to the golf course. I hit a bucket of practice balls and putted a little. I then went to the bar to have a few drinks before we started to play. The event was held in August and the temperature was above one hundred degrees. I really did not care because I got drunker than a football bat. I was the plant manager's third player, reason being no one knew how well I played. I played damn good considering I was drunk. We finished third. We won fifty dollars apiece. I think we would have done much better if I had not been drunk but we did win more money than we invested besides I played better than my captain did even in my condition. The plant manager told me that he was impressed with my golf game; however, he was not happy that I was so drunk. I had to agree with him and I promised him that would be the last time it would occur. The first year that I participated there was only seven teams but the number of teams increased through the years. We had the steak dinner at another player's home and I think the meal was good, I do not remember that much. I know I only drank tea. This was the only time I played drunk before or during a round of golf. I probably embarrassed myself and I did not want to have any excuses for a bad round. I have played with hangovers but not drunk. There were quite a few times that I wished I had been drunk but one time was enough.

When I met, "Leroy" he asked me if I played any sports. I told him that I played golf. He said we should play sometime and I said that would be great. He asked me a week later if I would like to play after work and I said o.k. He was not very good when we first began playing because he only swung the club with his arms, he did not use his lower part of his body. He could shoot in the nineties but at the time I did not care what he shot, all I cared about was that he enjoyed playing the game that I loved and that we worked together. I did not have to go out to find a game. We played for the fun of the sport not for money, well not a lot of money maybe a dollar for eighteen holes. "Ted" and "Roscoe" wanted to learn how to play golf. I asked them if they had ever played before and if they had their own clubs. They answered yes to both questions. "Leroy" and I said we were playing on Friday and they were welcome to join us. This was probably one of the biggest mistakes that "Leroy" and I ever made together. "Ted" and "Roscoe" were bad golfers, they not only did not know how to play but they did not know the etiquette of the game. The two of us were never so mad and embarrassed in our entire lives. I think it took us five hours to play that day. Between the two of them, I know they almost destroyed the whole course. They drove over roped off areas, drove too close to the greens and looked for golf balls as if they only brought one to play the with for the entire game. When we finished playing, I told them that they could not play golf with us any more until they had learned the rules and etiquette of the game. I handed each of them a rule book and told them when they had read the book and understood it then they could play golf with us again. I was proud that we had finished without them killing anyone or us killing them. "Leroy" and I played golf almost every Friday, completing our round in about three and a half hours. I tried to tell him that if he swung with his legs, he would get more distance but he would not listen. I once saw him hit a five wood over a tree about fifty yards in front of him onto the green another seventy yards away. The tree was at least fifty foot tall. We had a lot in common. We enjoyed each other's company, we played golf and we liked to party.

Once "Ted" and "Roscoe" had read the rule book we returned for another try. Their scores did not improve much but their manners improved drastically. "Leroy" and I actually were able to play another nine holes. "Ted" and "Roscoe" started to improve because they could not play much worse. "Ted" asked me how he could improve his game. I asked him if he worked out with weights often. He said that he lifted weights about four times a week. I told him to cut back a little for example instead of doing twenty reps of a certain weight do ten.

I told him that by reducing the number of repetitions that he would gain more flexibility in his golf swing. It would also allow him to develop a full turn in his swing. I said that lifting weights was fine, but too much lifting would throw your timing off and in golf, timing is everything. I said that if he intended to take golf seriously, he needed to practice. I said that by practicing with every club that you have he would develop the knowledge of how far that he could hit each club. I told him to practice until he hated to practice then practice some more. He did as I instructed him to do and to his surprise, he improved. I also told him not to tell anyone that he was playing golf and at the next company golf outing I would pick him for my team. True to my word when the company outing came, I chose him for my team. Every one of the captains started to laugh until they saw me smile and then they knew that I had been working with him on his game. Our team won the outing without much of a challenge from the other teams. "Ted" was so excited not just, because we had won but that he had helped the team. We won some money and some other prizes, plus we had our picture taken and it was put on the bulletin board at both plants. My team was elated about winning but all I wanted was the money and the trophy. A lot of the floor employees liked playing golf with management because this gave them a chance to kiss some major ass. I liked playing golf with them to prove that I was better than 98% of them and I was as good a human being not a retard like they thought. I know that most of management considered me as a dumb and stupid employee who took up a healthy person's job. Management soon realized I was smarter than they thought and this made them very unhappy that I could beat them at anything. Management soon realized that I was not playing in these outings to kiss their butts. I was there to win. The regular employees soon realized that one day does not make a year. Management considered they were better than the floor employees and treating us as equals for one lousy day was suppose to show that this was their way of letting us know that we were important to the company. I always thought that this was a lot of crap. The funny thing about all of this was that most of management did not know how to play golf. Lesser management was there for one reason only to kiss butt. This was really a big joke to me. These people had fancy cars, nice homes and a good paying job yet they were trying to play golf to impress their boss. I referred to this as idiots on parade. Someone not connected with the company would think he was watching Three Stooges shorts. I rarely chose a management player to play on my team. I tried to pick friends because even though we did not always win, we did have fun.

I remember one time my team consisted of "Leroy", "Ted", "Hans" and a woman. This woman was not interested in winning money she only wanted the trophy. She was very attractive. I will refer to her as hot pants because that is what she wore that day. The men would hit their shots from the men's tee then we would hurry to the women's tee and park on the left side because hot pants was right handed. She had this sexy way of teeing up her golf ball. "Ted" and I were married but we were not dead or crazy. She knew we were watching she did not care. I know that she was trying to inspire us to play our very best. If that was the reason, she accomplished her objective. We won the outing by three shots. It was also the first time a team had finished in double figures. Hot pants had achieved her goal, she received her trophy, and she said that the money was not important to her. I said go ahead take the money, the trophy and the cash were a matched set. The funniest thing about this story was that "Hans" did not understand why we parked our carts on the left side of the tee box before hot pants hit her shot. He asked "Leroy" at the dinner why we had done this. We told him that we enjoyed the way she placed the ball on the tee. He said that he was shocked and surprised at us because we were supposed to be honorable men. We told him that she knew what we were doing. We told him that if he did not approve he could kiss our butts, besides what was he griping about we won. We also told him that if she did not inspire him to play better that it was his fault not ours.

I remember one match that I played against a Stupidvisor who thought he would challenge me, to prove that his game was better than mine was. One morning when I was cleaning the break room, he cleverly asked if I would like to play him for money. "Leroy" and a few management people who also played golf were there listening. He said that he heard that I was good and we should get together to play very soon but he said that he would require some strokes in order to make the match even. I said I do not give anyone shots until we have played at least once. He then asked me what my handicap was to see if our games were similar. I was working overtime that morning and I was tired and sleepy. I also was an asshole. I said that my handicap was cerebral palsy in my right side. The other people who had been listening to the conversation started laughing hysterically. He was very embarrassed and stormed out of the break room madder than a disturbed hornet. I laughed to myself and continued my job. He was teased about the incident for weeks from management and some employees. We finally played the match and even though I caught him attempting to cheat, I still collected fifty dollars from him. He never challenged me to another golf match.

Another time, a boss considered his game to be so improved that he could give me a competitive match. I tried to tell him that he was not good enough, though he was getting better, to play me for money. I said that he should play "Ted" first then "Leroy" and if he beat them, I would consider his proposition. He said that he wanted to play against me now. I said that I would think about this challenge and I would let him know later. I returned about an hour later and told him that i did not think the match could happen because in my opinion he was not ready. He called me chicken and strongly insisted. I said that I would play against him but we had to play by the rules, except for the following rules he could use whenever he wanted. I said that I would give him fifteen shots for eighteen holes, two mulligan a side (for those people that do not follow golf a mulligan is a do over if a person hits a bad shot) and a throw a side. The bet would be twenty dollars to the winner. He agreed to these terms and we set up the match to be played at a course of my choosing. The match would take place on the next Friday. The day arrived and we met at a golf course in Chattanooga, "Leroy" and "Ted" came to watch the fun. The first hole was a par 5 easily reachable in two shots if a person could hit the ball reasonably long. I had to play the hole as a three shot hole because there was a pond in front of the green. The boss could reach the hole in two if he hit the ball straight. He pulled his second shot left of the green. I was getting ready to hit my third shot when he yelled to me that he was going to use one of his throws. I said go ahead. I should stop hear to explain that a golf ball is small. It is not like throwing a baseball or a football. A person can throw those balls overhand. A golf ball should be thrown underhanded or at least side-arm. The boss threw the ball as hard as he could towards the green. "Leroy" and I heard his arm pop 100 yards away. I turned to my friend and quietly stated "match over". I wanted to laugh but did not because he was in a lot of pain. I think I shot 75 and he shot 105. I gave him a putt on the last hole that was thirty feet long. When we had finished he said to me that I knew if he threw the ball overhand that he would get hurt. I said yeah but sometimes a person needed to learn lessons the hard way least they forget. I also told him not to make bets unless you have a chance to win, if you feel that a player is as good as you go ahead, play for a little cash. I think he learned a valuable lesson that day or at least a painful one.

I need to take the time to explain how the teams were chosen for the company golf outings. Basic course rules were to be observed for things like out-of-bounds, lost ball and water hazards. We did play everything as fairway except for sand traps. We played everything as fairway for two good reasons, to play quicker and to eliminate cheating. A team could improve their position one club length no closer to the hole. The first ball in the hole was the score for the team on that hole even though i do not think the rule was enforced. The teams were chosen two weeks before the outing. The captain of the team was considered the a player. It was his responsibility to explain the rules to his team and give out the gift bags. There was a lot of good things in these bags. There were shirts, two sleeves of balls, hats and tees plus some other things. The company always gave out cash prizes for the teams that finished among the top three with the lowest score. A prize was also given to the team with the worst score, usually a crying towel. The number of teams increased through the years as more people learned how to play golf. The first year that I played as I said before there was only seven teams, the last year that I played there was fourteen teams. We also moved the day of the event from Friday to Saturday in order to include the people from second shift. We did this because these people either could not play or had to take a day of vacation.

The teams were chosen in this manner. The a players was the captain of the team. He/she could shoot between seventy and eighty. They had the choice of which ball to play, the order the team was to play each shot and to keep score for his team. Most of the captains wanted to control their teams. I did not share their view, I thought that since this was a company outing, everyone should have a say about the way the team would play the hole. I remember this one guy who was hitting his tee shot on the third hole; he swung as hard as he could but missed the ball. He looked at me, expecting that I would say something to make him feel bad. I told him that it was all right and said to try to hit it. I told him that we would not be able to play his shot but it would not hurt anything or anyone for him to make another attempt. I told him to relax and hit the ball. He hit the ball down the middle of the fairway. He had a smile on his face the size of texas. He played better the rest of the day. He expressed to me that when he played in his first company outing his captain told him that he was the worst player that he had ever seen. I told him not to worry about some idiots heartless comments and enjoy the day. We finished third that day, I do not believe that I have ever seen such a big smile on anyone's face before or since in my life. I discovered later who his captain had been and I told the man that he did not have any class and that he should keep in the back of his mind that one day someone might think the same thing about him. I really felt like knocking him on his idiotic butt even though he was in management. I told him that if his personality did not change that I would embarrass him every chance I had the opportunity. I believe he got the message.

B players scored between eighty-five and ninety-five. They helped the captain quite a lot. They had some kind of weakness in their game whether it was iron shots putting etc. The captain depended upon them because the team could not win the event without their help.

C players scored between ninety-six and one hundred twenty. These players could do one thing exceptionally well. They would help the team when the captain would least expect the help.

D players were usually playing for the first time or they only played once or twice a year. They only wanted to score major points at work and kiss butt. The captain usually had to show them which way to hit the ball. I believe most of them were there to get a tan. Every once in awhile though, they contributed by making a putt or two. The teams and the people that I played with during these outings, were good people and I had a great time win or lose. There were however a few exceptions.

One particular time during a golf outing my team was playing awful. We were only two under par after nine holes. The day was going bad enough but two members of the team argued after every shot. "Roscoe" and I were playing the event by ourselves. I told them before we started playing the second nine holes if I heard another word spoken by them to each other, it had better be something nice or they could go home. I was feeling the effects of partying the previous night and I was sick and tired of their bickering. I told them I could hear that at home, I did not want to hear it now. They promised to stop bickering and concentrate on golf. I said that I would appreciate the effort. We began play on number 10, the longest par four on the golf course. The first player hit his ball out-of-bounds, the second player hit his ball to the ladies tee and "Roscoe" hit his ball onto the interstate. I had to hit the ball in bounds past the ladies tee but also far enough for the team to make at least a par. I will be the first person to admit that I make Fred Funk look like Tiger Woods as far as driving the ball a long way. I had a headache from partying the night before and I did not get any sleep the previous night. I was not having a good time especially playing golf with the bickering brothers. I started to tee up my ball and right before I hit my shot, they said in unison to hit a good shot. I slowly turned around and said that if I did then they would have to play a great deal better than they were doing up to this point. They said that they would try. I said that would be fine. I think I hit the longest and the straightest drive I have ever hit. The team made a par on the hole, then we birdied 7 out of the next 8 holes to finish nine under par and we won the golf outing. I told the team that we could have played better if the bickering brothers had acted like adults. The team who was playing behind us and had waited on every shot on the front nine holes thought we had quit, because they had lost sight of our team, we had left them far behind us. I asked "Roscoe" after the round was finished what the bickering brothers had said before I hit my tee shot on the tenth hole. He said that they were not worried because they had the best captain that was playing in the outing. I thought that if they knew how I felt that they might have panicked, because I felt like I had finished third in a two man hatchet fight. The team had performed well when matters counted that day and we won. I guess it was an o.k. day.

"Leroy", "Ted", "Roscoe" and I were playing golf in Chattanooga one Friday after work. Everything was going fine until we arrived at number 5. "Ted" and I had to hit our third shots over the water so I hit my shot first and returned to the cart to wait on him to hit his shot. He proceeded to hit his shot in the water and he got upset. I do not know why he got upset; the ball could have been new or it might have been that the rest of us were laughing. He threw his club towards the cart. The problem was that I was sitting in that cart and his club hit me in the shin, the dent that the club made in my shin remains today, some fifteen years later. I wanted to whip his butt but realizing that he was bigger and stronger than I was I used my better judgment and remained in the cart. I got even several years later, I hit him in the face with a plastic tray that brought blood, but he got the last laugh that day.

"Leroy", "Hans" and I were playing golf in Dalton Georgia one afternoon playing the eighteenth hole attempting to finish before dark. "Hans" hit a decent tee shot, flubbed his second shot then hit his third shot onto the green about thirty feet from the hole. He made the putt and started jumping up and down shouting birdie three times at the top of his lungs. The problem was that he had made a par. "Leroy" and I were laughing so hard that it took us about five minutes to tell him his correct score. We could not believe our ears when he told us that we were lying. We said that we would review each of his shots on the hole and let him decide who was telling the truth. He said that was fine by him. He realized he had forgotten his terrible second shot. He tried to say that shot did not count. We said that it did count because the ball had advanced about thirty yards. We told him that he had made an excellent par but the disappointment on his face was priceless.

"Ted" was improving about every time he played and he decided that he was going to see if he could be an a player in the next company golf outing. The outing director agreed because the outing needed captains badly. "Ted" had one condition though he had to pick first. He chose all of my picks so I had other team mates. My team did not win but we did better than "Ted's" team. My team finished fourth but his team finished last. His team received a crying towel. He learned a lesson that day, he was not ready to be a captain. I did not win money all the time but most of the time my teams did win money. I had fun playing golf with the employees, stupidvisors and management. The outing director passed away recently and it was because of him that the golf outings were so good. I heard that they do not have the outings anymore and I think that is sad. The outings brought the company closer together as a group and the outing gave the floor employees something to look forward to doing along side management. It would be a shame if the company did not include the golf outings in their budget but this is my opinion.

CHAPTER EIGHT

Chloe

I have to say that everything that I have done in my life with a few exceptions up to this point I had not been ashamed of myself. I disappointed my parents when I did not finish college but neither did my sisters and I did go to work and support my wives. My dad once told me that as long as I do not kill anyone in cold-blood or become gay, then he would stand behind me no matter what I did. I thought that was damn nice of him to make that statement. I always felt justified about everything that I did. I broke the law from time to time but luckily, no one was hurt except me. The one thing that I am ashamed about was my affair with Chloe.

Our relationship began very innocently. I met her soon after I had become an employee. She was working in shipping and I was a janitor. She stated that if I worked hard and did a good job then I would be recalled when production started to increase. She was right. I was laid off just before Christmas and recalled the first of March. I did not see Chloe for a couple of years because I was working at the packing plant, while she worked at the other plant. I was transferred to the plant that she was working. She had been replaced on her old job by someone else and ended up on third shift. When I walked into the plant, she saw me and walked up to me, and gave me a hug. I smiled and said that it was nice to see her.

Chloe had come from a good home. Her mother worked at XYZ Battery Company but I do not know what her dad did for a living. Her brother had worked there briefly, but he was fired when a stupidvisor claimed he was asleep. The stupidvisor was known to make up stories to get people dismissed. I never believed he was treated fairly but this is my opinion. Chloe got married right after high school so she could leave home. I believe that her parents were strict. I think that she married the first guy that asked her. He had a flashy car and she was easily impressed. I think she told me she was married to him for about nine months. Her next relationship was with a Stupidvisor at the Battery Company. He was married and had children. I do not know how long the affair lasted, but he did end it when they were almost discovered in the act. She then met a man working for the company and they were soon married. They had two children, a boy and a girl. He quit his job at the Battery Company for reasons I do not know and never cared to ask. He later took a job as a repairman in a housing project. He also sold drugs on the side for additional income but he used more than he sold. Chloe would then have to work overtime when the idiot would do this so she could pay the bills and keep the house.

She was probably my closest friend at the time outside of "Leroy". We talked before work, while I was getting my supplies and cleaning the women's rest room. We would share a cigarette while I waited for the floor to dry. She knew that I was single and that I was planning to remarry but I did not love this woman but it is better than being alone. She told me about her husband's drug dealings in front of the children, how she felt about working overtime all the time and that her family life sucked.

She came to work with a troubled look on her face and I asked her what was wrong. I wish now that I had not inquired about her problem but I did. She said that her husband's son from a previous marriage was touching their daughter in places where he should not be touching. I asked her what she intended to do about the problem. She said that she did not know what to do. I told her to go home and tell her husband that his son was doing bad things to their daughter. She asked me what she should do if he does not believe her. I told her to have her daughter tell him what his son was doing to her. She thanked me and departed. The next night she said that she had told her husband what his son was doing to their little girl. He did not believe her so the daughter told him the same thing. He did not believe her either. I told her to take her to a doctor to have her examined. If the doctor confirmed that their daughter was being molested then your husband could not deny that his son was not doing bad things to their daughter. She took my advice and had her examined. The doctor said that he noticed some bruising in that area but the husband still did not believe that his son would do such a thing. I believe that he was stoned out of his mind and could not comprehend anything that was being said. I told her to go home and tell the dumb SOB that his son could not return to their home and that the only way he could see his son was to visit him at his house. She said that she was afraid of him because he had pushed her down while she was pregnant with their son. I told to tell him that he had to make a choice; the son from his first marriage or the children that he had with you. I said to her that if he hits you call the police and take the kids and go to your parents house. I think that suggestion worked because when she arrived at work she was smiling and said that everything was fine. I found out later that his son from the first marriage was having emotional problems because his mom and dad had divorced. He thought that the problem was he and he was trying to get attention from his dad. I heard that he did receive counseling. I did not hear any more about him after that particular episode.

One night my boss asked me to work on Friday night to strip the cafeteria floor. I told him that we did not have enough people to get the job done in eight hours because the other people that worked in my department were 60 years old. I asked him if I could ask someone else to help. He said did I have anyone in mind. I suggested Chloe. He asked me if I had asked her yet and I said no I have not but she could use the overtime. He told me to go ahead and ask her if she would not mind helping us out and he told me that I would be in charge of the job. I told him that the other ladies would not be happy because they had more seniority that I did. He said for me to go and find them and tell them to come to see him. I said I would do that and then I would ask Chloe if she wanted to work Friday night. I figured that she would because we had a good friendship and her family needed the money. I asked Chloe if she had any plans for Friday night and when she said no, I asked her if she would like some overtime helping my crew strip the break room floor. She said that she would be glad to help and thanked me for asking. I told her to be here by ten o'clock because we had to empty the break room of all the tables and chairs and that would take awhile because we would not get much help from the rest of the crew. I told her that we had to be finished by six o'clock because the powder room was supposed to work on Saturday. She said she would see me that night. I told my boss that she was going to be able to help us out and he said that was fine. He said that he had told the other ladies you were going to be in charge of the project and that they started complaining until he told them that if a mistake was made or the floor was not done to his satisfaction they would be held responsible. He said the complaining stopped quickly. I asked him if he had told them not to sabotage the job. He said that he had not given that possibility much thought but would discuss this issue with them when he saw them later that night. I told him that I would appreciate the warning to the ladies because they thought that I was your pet and that you treated me better than they did. He told me that he did like me better but he knew I would get the job done while they would stand and argue over something petty. Everyone arrived on time and the tables and chairs were removed from the break room. I had brought my radio and turned it to a country music station, when the older ladies began to complain about my choice of music. I asked them what type of music they would like me to have on the radio and they said gospel. I said next time you bring in your own radio and then you can chose the type of music. I said that I liked gospel but not at work. This would be the first of many arguments that would occur that night. The floor was stripped and mopped so we had some time before we had to apply the first coat of sealer. The ladies went into the women's restroom while I stood guard to make sure no one entered the break room. Everything was proceeding quite nicely until about 2:00 in the morning. I think that at that time all hell descended on my location. The ladies said that I was doing everything wrong. I reminded them that the boss had placed me in charge and that they were going to do things my way or they could leave and I would explain to the boss in the morning why they were not there. I should not have said anything because it just made things worse. The ladies started bitching at me as if I was the devil himself and I thought that this would be a great time to take a break. I threw my mop across the room, told the crew to take a ten-minute rest while I cleared my head. I left the break room and instead of going into the men's restroom, I went to the women's because they had a couch to sit on while I figured out what to do about the problem I was having with those bickering ladies. Suddenly without warning, I felt a hand on my left shoulder as I entered the restroom. It was Chloe and before I could say anything, she put her arms around me and gave me the longest, deepest and wettest kiss I had ever had in my entire life. This action caught me completely by surprise. She said that she had wanted to kiss me for a very long time but thought that this action would ruin our friendship. I said that if you can repeat the same kiss then I would believe you. She kissed me again and the kiss was better than the first. I think that I was in shock or heaven I could not distinguish between the two at that time. This is how my love affair with Chloe started.

We got the floor done in the allotted time and the job was done well. My boss was pleased and he asked me if everyone had gotten along. I said in front of the ladies that had given me so much trouble that night that everything had been done without any bickering or confusion. I went home that morning feeling a little confused. I was brought up believing that a person did not have a relationship with a woman who was married. Chloe and I stayed close together the rest of the night. I lived in another city, I did not have a phone and I still was dating someone else who thought I was going to marry her. The next night I was supposed to give her an engagement ring. I took her out to dinner that night and told her that I had met someone else. I could not see the both of them and I now know I should not have been seeing either of them. I knew that I broke her heart and I felt bad about hurting her. She was a wonderful person and deserved a better person that would treat her with respect. I took her home after dinner and kissed her on the cheek. I told her that I hoped she had a good life. She slapped my face and said that she wanted me. I just said good-bye walked to my car and drove away. I do not regret breaking off the engagement because I do not believe that the marriage would have lasted but I do regret hurting her. I spent the remainder of the weekend thinking about Chloe, what if anything would happen Sunday night.

The answer to my question came quickly on Sunday night when Chloe arrived for work. She approached me and gave me a big hug, right in the middle of the plant in front of God and everyone. I was surprised because I did not expect anything to happen. I was very much mistaken. She met me in the lady's room next to the break room. She gave a big hug and a deep kiss. I told her that I had broken up with the other woman and then I asked her what was next for us. She said that she wanted to have sex with me. I said when would she like to do it and more importantly where? She said as soon as possible and that she would choose a date that was convenient for both of us. She said that she would give the matter some thought and let me know. I saw her later and she said what about this Friday. I told her that would be fine with me and so the date was set. She asked me on Friday how to get to my apartment and I gave her directions. She also asked me to pick up some condoms. I said that I would pick up some on my way home. I could not find any though I looked several different places. She came to my apartment later that morning and she said that we were going to have sex like never before. I told her that I could not find any condoms. She said that she did not care and I said fine. We had passionate sex for three hours non-stop. It was the best sex I had ever experienced. It was simply great. I did not want the time we were spending together to end. She had to go home before her husband returned home from work and she had to pick up her son from kindergarten. I took a shower, then went to bed and slept like a baby.

I could not wait to get to work the next Sunday night. I arrived at work thirty minutes early, she was already there waiting for me. We talked about last Friday's proceedings and if she wished to continue. She said that she wanted to see me again. I stated that I had no problem with her idea. We became a couple at work. I talked to her whenever possible and I did have a job to perform. I did most of my job quickly except while cleaning the women's restroom where we would meet to share a hug and a few kisses. The first few weeks we took our breaks at different times but after awhile we took our breaks together with her best friend whose name I can not recall.

When we started our affair, we were two large people. We decided to go on a diet together. I weighed almost 300 pounds and she about 250 pounds. The day we decide to end the diet she had lost 100 pounds and I had lost over 110 pounds, making me weigh about 185.

She told her best friend what was going on between her and me. I told "Leroy". This many people knowing about us did not bother me at all but other people discovered bits and pieces and made up everything else. The news of our love affair spread like a wildfire in California. The employees were talking about us and who was going to be brave enough to inform her husband what his wife was doing with a another employee.

We agreed to deny any involvement and I decided to spread the word that unless any one could prove the affair was going on or if they had pictures, then it would be in their best judgment to stop this gossip or I would complain to the personnel office. This action by me stopped all the rumors, I was thankful no one called my bluff. We soon returned to our activities hotter than before.

My friends said that after a round of golf that they wanted to talk to me about my relationship with Chloe. I asked "Ted" and "Roscoe" how they knew about Chloe and me. They said that "Leroy" had told them. He said that they were your friends too, and besides they knew something was going on because you had not played golf for a while. I said that I was not mad with him I just wish he had told me. We went to our favorite watering hole and after we had consumed a few beers and I had a couple of drinks, they all said that it was alright to have sex with her but not to fall in love with her. I said I would take their advice, but it was too late, I was falling hard and this would cost me later. I would not have listened to them anyway because if all four of my friends and I had one thing in common it was that we were all stubborn.

Our involvement with each other increased. We would arrive at work before any one else. The Thanksgiving weekend holiday we met at a service station and made out like a bunch of teenagers. I gave her my parents telephone number in case she needed to talk to me. During the Easter holidays I went to my parents house because I could play golf with my dad and eat my mom's great cooking. I could have gone to Florida but I could play golf at my parent's golf course for free. She telephoned me every other day because she claimed that she was lonely. She finally asked me to return home but I told her that I promised my parents I would stay until Sunday morning. She started to cry and I said that I would see her as soon as I could. She said that she would look forward to that day.

We started to plan our meetings with more precision. We had to be extra careful because of the rumors; we did not want to be caught and lose our jobs or have her husband discover what was happening. I still lived in another city so I had made a reservation at a local hotel in the town where she lived. She had taken her children to her parent's house and told them that she was going shopping that day. She arrived shortly after I had showered. We had a wonderful day. Sex, sex, sex all day then we would talk for a little while then have more sex. I thought the day was moving in slow motion, hoping the day would last forever. She was fantastic in bed. Every time I see Porky's (the movie) I think of her because she was a moaner. There was more than one time that while we were having sex, someone would bang on the wall or I would receive a call from the front desk asking me if I was having a party. I would say no but I would turn down the television. We would share a laugh and return to having sex.

She finally asked me to move to her town so we could spend more time together. I said that I would after the first of the year. She showed up at my apartment unexpectedly on New Year's Eve. I was going out partying with three friends of mine from work. We had rented a room at the Choo-Choo in Chattanooga so we could party without worrying about police roadblocks because we were going to use a taxi to travel around town. I really did not understand her sometime she had left her daughter in the car while we were inside my apartment having sex. I felt sorry about her kid being left in the car but this did not bother Chloe so I guess it was all right. She said that she wanted me to know she did not care if I partied and danced with another girl but she did not want me to have sex. I looked at her with a puzzled expression and said that she was probably going to have sex, why could I not have sex. She said that she was married. I wish she had not said those words because that weird feeling began to return. I wondered what was I doing having sex with a married woman. She then said something very unexpected; she said that she was in love with me. This remark hit hard, I asked her to say it again because I did not think I heard her right. She repeated what she had said before. She kissed me good-bye and said I will see you next year. I started to think that what I was doing was wrong but I was in too deep. I loved her too.

I returned to work after the holidays and told Chloe that I had fulfilled my lease and I would be moving to her town soon. I moved into a hotel not far from work that was reasonable. I had a place to sleep a bathroom, a telephone, a TV and a small refrigerator. I was able to see Chloe 3 to 4 times a week. I took my dirty laundry to the dry cleaners, which cost $15.00 A week. I loved the arrangement. I could see my girl, live near work, receive a wake-up call, life could not be better. I thought so anyway but I was wrong, again.

I said that at the beginning of the chapter that when we began our affair we were both overweight. I used illegal drugs. I do not know how she did it but if I thought about it for a second I would figure out how. I did figure it out I was not the only man besides her husband that she was having sexual relations. I knew because they told me. I informed her that these men who I had trusted told me that she was having sex with them and if that were true, we were through. She promised she would stop and stupid me believed her. I figured out that she was looking for a better situation for herself and her children.

I had told my boss of the affair because I knew that he would tell me if trouble was coming my way. We did have sex at work a couple of times when she was helping me but I am not going into details because this could affect other people who still work for XYZ Battery Company.

Chloe and I could not spend a lot of time talking at work during the week because we had jobs we had to get done and the people who spread gossip. The older women were mainly the people who spread gossip throughout the plant. I think they place it on their job application as a sport or hobby. Chloe and I came up with a solution we exchanged letters. I am not saying that she was dumb but she could not spell worth a damn. She wrote me a letter one morning asking me if I would be able to see her later that day or was I going to play golf. She said that it was up to me but let her know weather I wanted to play golf or be with her. I read the letter and when i got to that part of the letter, I started laughing. I laughed so hard I doubled over having to sit on the floor to keep from falling down. She got mad. I explained to her the reason why I was laughing she got even madder. I told her I was going to play golf. She acted hurt. It is still funny to me every time I think about it when I remember the letter.

I use to give her gifts, not expensive gifts because I did not want to raise any suspicion from her husband. He was an idiot but he was not that stupid. I would give her sweat shirts with her favorite college team's logo on the front, just stuff like that would make her happy. One time though I did buy her a ruby ring with small diamonds encircling the ruby. It was worth $350.00. I gave the ring to her at work in a beautiful box neatly wrapped. I said do not open this until I was out of sight. She said that she would wait. I gathered my supplies for the evening's work and left. I did not return to her area until two hours later. She had tears in her eyes and said that was the nicest gift anyone had ever given her. I smiled and told her that I loved her. I had just made a big mistake!!! She knew that she could ask me to do anything for her (short of murder) and I would do it for her. She said that she loved me too but in a different tone of voice than usual.

I am a little naïve when it comes to women. I did not think that I was committing adultery because I was not married. I was a complete moron. I wanted her to obtain a divorce so we could marry and start a life together. She said that she would love to but it would have a bad effect on the children. I told her that if you were not happy with your husband it did not matter because your children were not happy either. I do not believe in divorce but I am not going to remain in an unhappy relationship just for the sake of the children especially if they are small. I said that if a person is unhappy and can better their selves by leaving a spouse that is either sleeping, fucked up on drugs all the time and demanding sex whenever he feels the need then for the sake of the children that person should move on with their life. She said that she would give the matter some thought. I said that was fine.

One day, a short time later while I was at my parents house she dropped in unexpectedly accompanying her was her daughter. They were returning home from a Majorette Competition. She had already talked to my mom and Chloe wanted them to meet the woman that their son was dating. She stayed for a few hours and since I was leaving to return home, she followed me home. I had been home for my quarterly pep talk. The, Pete you should return to college and get your degree in speech so you can be in management speech. I tried to explain to them that I did not want to be a Stupidvisor for XYZ Battery Company because they lose their jobs on a whim. My mom said that I should get a degree so

I could teach school. They were right about that, I should have done what they had requested. I was too stubborn though to give the matter any consideration.

Chloe and I started to drift apart soon after. We had delivered some product for her husband and I became very upset. I told her that we could have been caught and gone to jail. She asked me if I was afraid. I said hell yeah I was scared I had no plans for going to jail and losing my job. She said that I was not the man that she thought I once was and I told her I was not stupid, and if her idiot husband wanted to make some money, he should make the delivery the next time.

My parents were in Chattanooga to play in a golf tournament and they asked me to bring Chloe to meet their friends. I asked her to go and we went but I realized that something was wrong. She would not say what was bothering her. We visited with them for a time but I told them it had been a long night and we had to get back home. We did not talk the entire way home. I dropped her off at her car and as I was pulling away she said that we had to cool things for a little while because someone had called "Kevin" and told him that she was having an affair with this fat guy from work. He told her to stop the affair if it was happening or this fellow would meet a premature death. I told her he could not pick me out of a line-up of balding men even if I was the only person in the line-up with a full head of hair. I agreed to her request.

She did come to my apartment on my birthday. We had great sex that day. She stayed three hours or more but the distance was growing wider everyday.

There is one story I would like to tell that I waited until now to share. Chloe came to my hotel room for a social call with her 2 year old son. She said that she had wanted to have sex with me so badly that she was willing to take the risk by bringing along her son. I had two beds at the hotel where I was staying. She laid him down for his nap in one bed and after he fell asleep, we had sex in the other bed. Soon after we had gotten dressed, he woke up from his nap. I played hide and seek with him until it was time for them to leave. He had brought some toy golf clubs with him and I showed him how to hit the ball. He hit some plastic golf balls in my room. When they were leaving, she gave me a large glass bottle of green m&m's. I began to get a bad case of the guilt's for having sex with her, with her little boy in the bed next to us. I think I knew that the relationship was going to fail even though I did not want that to happen.

The last time that we had sex was in August of 1988. I knew her heart was not into it and frankly, mine was not either. I was using speed quite a lot, drinking a lot and gambling often. The entire time we were committing adultery. I thought that I had found the woman of my dreams. I was sadly mistaken; I was there until she could find someone better. I filled a void in her life. I was better that what she had but not as good as the person that she really wanted. Her reduction in weight had brought her to the attention of a Stupidvisor. He began to talk to her and filled her head with dreams of a far better life. He told her that he would only stick around if she obtained a divorce and that I was completely out of the picture. She told me that we were through and she would not be seeing me ever again. I was devastated.

I have heard that revenge is best when served cold. I asked that she return the ring that I had given her 6 months before. She said that she would like to keep the ring so she would have something to remember me by. I told her that if she did not want me then there was no reason for her to keep the ring. I said that she could keep all the shirts that I had given her to remember me because I did not like that school anyway. She wanted to keep the ring but she gave it back reluctantly. She knew how much I had paid for the damn thing. I placed it on my left pinkie finger and walked away. The story does not end hear, it gets much better. "Jezebel" the most hated stupidvisor in the plant, asked me in front of the window where I picked up my supplies if the ring was intended for anyone. I said no. She then asked me if I had any special attachment to the ring. I looked at Chloe and she at me again I said no. She asked me the cost of the ring and I said $350.00. She said that she would give me $150.00 For the ring. I looked at Chloe who was shaking her head no please do not sell the ring to her. I smiled and said that would be fine but I wanted cash. She said that she would bring the money the next night. I said that was fine with me and she could pick up the ring. Chloe called me over to her work station and asked me why I had sold the ring to the woman that I hated more than anyone in the entire world. I told her that someone new had replaced her. She inquired as to whom I was talking about and I said with a smile on my face, you babe.

I was glad that the affair had ended but sad in other ways. I knew that the affair was wrong but I let my little head think for my big head. The events that had transpired over the last eighteen months went against everything my parents had told me. My dad said that it was fine to look but do not touch. It did break my heart though because the person that she chose was a friend of mine. I guess all is fair in love and war. She kept calling me two or three times a week until they were married. They were married on a day when they knew that I would be out of town on a golf trip. I would not have tried to interfere with their wedding plans but I guess they did not want to take any chances. She still phoned me after they were married, at least for a while. "Leroy" "Ted" and her husband were going to Chattanooga to play golf one Friday after work when her husband asked who was going to be the fourth. "Leroy" said it was going to be Pete. "Ted" told me that he turned pale. During the company picnic, held at Dollywood, Chloe had seen me and "Alice" walking through the park hand in hand. She had practically run to see the person that had taken her place. "Alice" and I were married on March 2, 1991. This date was chosen for a reason. It was also her husband's birthday she always wanted something to remember her me by so I gave her such an occasion. She obtained her college degree through one of those accelerated programs. I heard she is pushing papers now but she is doing it alone. Her husband divorced her some time ago and "Alice" and I keep on celebrating our Anniversary every year.

This proves that an affair is not what people think it is going to be. A person needs to be willing to take the risk of becoming involved with another person before proceeding. I suggest that a person leads with his brain and not the heart or some other part of the body. Do not have children until the marriage is going to take. Children are often hurt emotionally when put in a bad situation by their parents. I urge anyone considering an affair to talk to someone first. Parents, a marriage counselor and if you still do not feel convinced then pray about the situation. I believe that you will receive an answer it might not be the answer that you want to hear but an answer will be received.

Chloe always told me that she got married the first time to get out of the house and the second time to have children and the third time for money. I wonder what the reason will be for the fourth time.

Looking back on my relationship with her, I regret that I lost her friendship. I know that I was planning to spend the rest of my life with her but we use to have a lot of great conversation. I miss those talks. I learned my lesson and that I am grateful. I give this warning to all the Chloe's of the world, please remember one thing. An affair works both ways if a man will cheat with you then he will cheat on you. Please be careful. This is a tough world.

CHAPTER NINE

How I Lost My Job

The end happened about seven years ago. It began at first break on the last night before summer vacation. My friends and I were having smoking a cigarette outside. We were talking about new jobs, which were being offered to the employees after summer vacation. One of the girls asked me if I was going to apply for any of the new positions. I replied no because since the only job I was qualified for was already filled, I was not going to apply for anything else. She asked me what job I was talking about. I said Plant Manager. We all got a good laugh about my statement, and then we returned to work. I did not notice the three temporaries that were also outside during break. (A temporary was a person that performed the same job as a regular employee but for lesser pay and no insurance benefits) the three temps, after break went to my supervisor and informed her that at break that I had referred to the Plant Manager as a n-----. My supervisor, who was new to the job, became very upset because she too was black. I have to say at this point that I am not now nor have I ever been a racist. I hope I have treated everyone equally. I tried to follow the golden rule. I do not like certain people but it is not because of their race, religion, disability or sexual orientation. I choose my friends very carefully because I do not seek pity or desire to make people feel guilty about my misfortune. I wish the world felt this way but it does not so I can only control what happens with me. My boss did not speak to me the rest of the night.

The shift was winding down; everyone was ready for a vacation when my boss came to my work area to tell me not to leave the plant when the shift had ended. I wondered why but I said that I would stay when the shift was over. The supervisor left and I continued to clean my work area because if I left an unclean work area the lady on day shift would kick my butt. I was taking my garbage back to the dumpster when my boss had returned to my work area. She went a little crazy asking my operator where I had gone. My operator informed her that I had to take my trash to the dumpster and I would be back shortly. The operator told my boss that he had to finish his job and that was a part of his job. She calmed down after she discovered that I was still inside the plant. When I had returned from discarding my trash, she said that I had to go and see "Elijah". He was in charge at the packing plant. I told my boss that I would go to his office as soon as my replacement arrived. When I was relieved, I went to "Elijah's" office. I entered his office and discovered not only him but also another person from management along with my boss who was crying. I inquired what the subject of this meeting. "Elijah" said for me to sit down. I said no thanks I will stand. He said that he had a question to ask me but it would not affect my job in any way. I tried to think what I might have done to be in trouble. I knew that I was in trouble because of the fact there were two big bosses and my boss in the office at the same time. When he said my answer to his question would not affect my job, I knew that he was lying. I knew that he was lying because his mouth was moving. I had to have done something very bad for that many big bosses to be assembled in the same office at one time. I knew my job was on the line if my answer was what they considered bad for the company. I told him to ask his question because I had nothing to hide. He asked me if I referred to the Plant Manager as the N word. I told him I said no such thing. I also told him that I respected the Plant Manager and enjoyed the fact that he was one of the best Plant Managers that XYZ Battery Company ever had in the position. I asked him who had said that I had used that word about the Plant Manager. He refused to say who the culprits were. He only said that the matter had been brought to the attention of my boss. I said that I have never used that word. I thought to myself that even if I had been the Grand Wizard of the Ku Klux Klan I knew where I worked and I was not that stupid to say the N word at XYZ Battery Company. I also told him that I had witnesses to back up my story. I told him to ask them what I said and they would give me an alibi. He told me to go get my witnesses but not to say anything about why they needed to report to the office. I went to the two ladies and told them that they needed to go to "Elijah's" office. They inquire why but I told them I could not say. I clocked out and waited in the parking lot. The two ladies were interviewed one at a time. Their stories were the same. I had not referred the Plant Manager the N word. They were thanked for their cooperation and were excused. The two ladies had said the same thing I had said, I did not use that word. The two ladies came out to the parking lot and I asked them if the Three Stooges wanted to see me. They replied no but I was not going to leave until I received an answer about my job. I went to "Elijah's office and he said that my witnesses had back up my story. He said to have a nice vacation but did not offer an apology. They never mentioned that they had made a terrible mistake.

I went straight to the other plant and spoke with the head of personnel at great length about the recent events. He telephoned "Elijah". He said that three temps who had told this lie had made the complaint. He said that they thought they could get me in trouble so I might lose my job and they would have a better chance of gaining full time employment. The personnel manager said that those temps would never be allowed to return to work for the company. I said that I wished to speak to the Plant Manager, which I did. He said that he believed my story and I should get on with my vacation. I left the plant a nervous wreck. Management never once said that they were sorry about the events which had occurred that morning. I arrived at home pissed as hell. "Alice" knew I was pissed off because my favorite baseball team was playing an afternoon game that day and I should take a nap so I could rest until it was time for the game. I said that I did not care about the damn game and I was too upset to sleep.

I do not believe I slept more than 40 hours the entire two weeks I was on vacation. I kept thinking about the accusation and especially no apology.

This is not the first time I had been harassed by management about things they were told that I had done. Someone said that

I used up the foam in the fire extinguishers. I did not know how to use one if I had been on fire myself. A person told a Stupidvisor accusing me of pulling a fire alarm, which brought the fire department to our plant. This turned out to be a false accusation because I had been in the restroom at the time. I told them that I would rather jump off the Empire State Building naked, than pull a stupid stunt like that particular one. The stunt that happened every time, I mean every time that I applied for a different job, I was sent to the rehabilitation center to see if I still had Cerebral Palsy. I told them on numerous occasions that Cerebral Palsy was a birth defect and my particular type was like a stroke. I tried to explain to them that all my muscles on my right side were underdeveloped. I could lift a tray of batteries or play golf because I used different muscles but as far as packing batteries into a box my fingers could not operate at the speed that they expected.

I even told them that all my organs on the right side of my body are smaller than my left. I guess they did not believe me.

The tests consisted of walking up and down steps, dexterity tests, carrying weights changing the number of pounds each time until I could not carry the weights anymore, crawling around on the floor, attempting to walk heel to toe which I could do with my left foot but not my right. My therapist would say that I had Cerebral Palsy. I would say no kidding I thought that I was faking. This event happened at least three time maybe more. I lost count of the times that I took this stupid test. I know that I took the test so many times that the man that administered the test started referring to each other on a first name basis. I can not count the number of times that management would ask me if I still had still had CP. They wanted to know if would ever disappear and I then I could to do a regular job. The first few times I tried to explain that CP was a birth defect and that I would have it for the rest of my life. The next one hundred times I would shake my head and walk away except when "Ted" asked me if I still had CP. I knew that his boss, who disliked me, had encouraged him to ask such a stupid question. I calmly told him that he was full of shit! I said that you had known me for 14 years and had he ever seen me walk normally, seen me do anything with my right hand or arm, anything that would lead him to change his opinion about my disability. He said that I was good at golf, almost the best in the company. I said first that the muscles that I used to play golf were very different muscles; second, I played more often than anyone else did and third most everyone else sucked. He started to say something else but I cut him off and said that he should have known better than to ask a stupid question, and then I walked away. He apologized later for having mentioned my disability but as I said before his boss had insisted that because we were friends his boss thought I would say something to "Ted" that I would not tell anyone else. I told him that he should have agreed to his bosses wishes and not mentioned it to me. He agreed with me and I told him that this incident had not harmed our friendship. I told him to tell them to kiss my southern ass but he said no. He would convey my sentiments in a different way.

When my vacation was over, I returned to work looking to make a fresh start putting the incident behind me hopefully moving forward. This did not happen. My boss wanted me to hear her side of the story. I said to her that I did not want to hear her side of the story and as far as I was concerned, the matter was over. I wanted to tell her to go to hell and stay away from me. I could not do that because management would have a good reason to get rid of me. She insisted and I said no! She kept after me until I thought I was going to lose my mind. I telephoned "Rita" and told her what was happening. I told her I thought I was going crazy. I was crying like a baby. I told her that my boss was insisting that I hear her side of the story about the events that transpired right before vacation and she refused to leave me alone. "Rita" told me to go home and that she would arrange for me some counseling. I informed my boss that I was leaving. She said that I could not go home because she did not have a replacement to take my place. I said that I did not care and if she had a problem with my leaving then she should call "Rita", and then I went home. The next day I saw a psychologist and I broke down.

I never heard of a nervous breakdown before but the psychologist said that I had all the symptoms of one. I could not sleep, did not want to eat, cried uncontrollably for no reason at all, and did not want to be around anyone or do anything. I wanted to hurt those people who had hurt me. The truth is that I still do but there are no golf courses in prison. I have always tried to treat people the way I wanted to be treated. This did not happen because there were too many idiots, dumb butts, tattletales, and uneducated dweebs to deal with and I am not even including management. I think most of the people that worked at XYZ Battery Company were members of the Nazi Party. Employees and management alike would sell out their best friend to better their position at the company.

My recovery was very slow. I started to hear voices. I slept 3 hours a night. I constantly considered killing those people that had questioned my disability. It took me about two years before I was willing to try to return to work. Management said that they had made a job just for me. The job would involve no one else, I would be the boss. I guess I could say that I would be the Stupidvisor. I returned to work with the intention of starting my new job. Management had lied to me again. I was shocked! (I was not really just seeing if you were paying attention). My job was sorting caps and nails to see if they were the correct size. They made my work area directly in front of the break room. I thought that this was the worst place for me to perform my job. I was in close contact with the people who had made me have a nervous breakdown in the first place. The first few days went surprisingly well. Chloe found out that I had returned to work and she made a special trip over to the plant where I was working to see me. I started to lose control. My doctors had told me that if I felt a panic attack coming I should get up and walk around until the symptoms began to subside. Chloe was my triggering mechanism; the attacks became more frequent. The final straw that broke the camel's back was when a Stupidvisor told me to sit my fucking ass in my chair and do my job. I wanted to tell him to go visit his relatives in hell but I did not say a single word. I went to the nurse and she sent me home. I returned to work after Thanksgiving in 1999. Everyone was worried because people thought everything would change at the end of this year. Their fears were realized when it became a

New Year. Management placed me on second shift, a shift they knew I did not like. This was not the worse thing that happened though; I was put with a bunch of bible thumpers. (I am not talking about Christians; I am talking about people that might handle snakes, drink poison and have to be in church every time the door is open). They wanted me to attend prayer meetings, bible studies and attend their church. I was asked what denomination I was, what church I attended. I did not answer them. I felt that this was none of their business. They began to avoid me like the plague, I began to experience more panic attacks, and I felt very depressed.

My stupidvisor was a Karate fanatic, a black belt I think but I am not sure. I started to feel more depressed and the panic attacks increased each day. I was hoping to make it to the Christmas holidays. I made it to the Christmas holidays by God's good graces. The employees that had to work the first week of Christmas vacation were getting ready to leave work for Christmas and the New Year holiday when a stupidvisor by the name of "Sporty" had to say something that he considered intelligent directed towards me. "Sporty's" true calling should have been a jockey. He was five feet tall and weighed 130 pounds soaking wet. He stated that no one here could hurt him physically except Pete. He thought that he was being funny but I just turned my head and suggested that he not laugh because it might happen. A sudden jolt of fear filled his eyes as I smiled.

My depression got worse with each passing day. The panic and anxiety increased. I did talk with one particular woman even though she was very religious we talked about other things. I told her that I was tired and desperate. She listened to my problems. I will always thank God for her listening to me.

The last night for me at XYZ Battery Company was a Thursday night. I had taken enough shit from the company. I considered committing suicide but that is a cop-out. I was sick and tired of being sick and tired. I told the nice lady that I would not return. The end of the shift did not arrive soon enough for me. The shift finally ended and I never looked back because even though I had pleasant memories, I had much more bad memories. It took 17 years but they finally got to me. I gave up trying to work within their system. The first few years were fun and enjoyable but due to all the added rules, the tests to see if I was faking CP, the write-ups and the false accusations I broke down. I returned to my doctors in worse shape than I had been before.

I applied for workman's compensation. They told me that a nervous breakdown was not a work related injury. I said that it was work related. They stated that they would investigate my case and I should call them the next day. I telephoned them and they said that they could not help me. I applied for Social Security Disability Insurance. I had to take tests to prove that I had Cerebral Palsy and they checked with my doctors. I was qualified to receive the Social Security Disability Insurance. I now had income, not close to the income that I was use to receiving but I had income. I must have fallen through the cracks because I received insurance for my wife and myself for about two years until they caught the mistake. My wife has no insurance at the this time, and I have Medicare.

I am slowly getting better. I no longer smoke every day because my wife quit cold turkey. I take four 10 milligrams of Valium every day and a blood pressure pill. I also use insulin twice daily. I still see "Leroy" or we talk at least once a week. I thought about suing XYZ Battery Company but I did not think I could handle court. The majority of the people I have named in the book no longer work with the company or have retired. I believe they are better off since they moved forward with their lives.

I am not cured nor do I think I will ever be cured. I still hold grudges against the people in the book that I did not like. I will do them no harm but if they should pass away, I will be smiling on the inside. Some people think I got what I deserved. I strongly disagree. I tried my best. Management did not believe that I had a physical handicap and their treatment towards me proves that this is a fact.

My true wish is that the company would go bankrupt. This event would make my millennium. I am still very angry but I feel I have a right and as Forest Gump said that is all I have to say about that.

CHAPTER TEN

Thoughts And Opinions

I have seen a lot of things that have been good for this country and some things that were not so good during my life. I am now offering my thoughts and opinions about what i have seen. These are my thoughts and opinions; you may agree with them or you may disagree, it does not matter.

I believe it is time for this country to stand as a country, not as 250 million individuals that only agree when something happens that is bad. It is time for the people to say enough is enough. The fighting among each other must stop. It is time to stand behind your chosen leaders and encourage them to lead the nation in the direction that will make this the best country in the world. It is time to quit acting like children, thinking the government is attempting to steal your freedom. It is time for this country to act as one nation under God and dedicated that no one is going to mess with us.

I know that everyone has a heritage to be proud of, but it is the time for every American to be proud to be an American first. It should not be Irish-American, African-American, Jewish-

American, etc. It should be just American. I am not saying a person should not be proud of where his ancestors originally lived before coming here, but what I am saying it is time to look at each other no matter what race, religion, or culture a person practices the bottom line is that we are all Americans. I do not look upon people that are not exactly like me with hatred or think they are treated better than I am, it is your God-given right to think differently, and that is why you have a brain. The bottom line is the next time you feel mistreated because of someone's color, think before you do anything that you might regret.

I believe that every child that went to high school or received their GED should do their damn best to go to college. If for some reason you are not ready to attend college then go into the military. This will enable you to learn a trade and after you have served your tour, you can reenlist or go to school. The time is coming when a person will need a degree to work just about anywhere.

I believe that more companies should hire handicap people because they have a lot to offer. All we want is a chance to be productive in society, most of us are willing to work but companies do not wish to take a chance because they think that we will screw up the works. This is not true. We would be on time, show up for work when we are suppose to be there and give a great deal of effort to make sure the company progresses to achieve the greatest possible success.

I believe that Jack Nicklaus and other Professional Golf Association Members that tried to keep Casey Martin from pursuing his life long dream ought to be ashamed of their actions because he cannot walk the golf course as they have to do. I believe this is a form of bias that is simply unfair. It is saying that if he cannot walk 18 and sometimes 36 holes in a day then he cannot play. I compare this to the saying "that if you do not want to play by my rules then I will take my ball and go home". I tell you what, the next time you play a practice round put some rocks in your shoes and play the entire round and then let me hear your opinion. You had a great gift, allow Casey to pursue his career. I have a better idea; start a tour for the handicap, call it the Golden Bear Tour. I think that it is about time that we had our own tour. This would be a great humanitarian thing for your image and the handicap golfers who I know there are plenty who can compete with their own kind.

I believe that is about time that all major sports dissolve their unions. Players sign contracts worth millions of dollars and yet you have the nerve to go on strike. This to the regular sports fan is not only selfish but also stupid. I believe that if a player signs a contract, is he suppose to honor that agreement. A player should feel very lucky to be playing a boy's game as a man. It is time to grow up! The union may had a purpose at one point but no more. The players must realize that if they strike again, I doubt if even the die-hard fans will, return and then what will you do for a living. I know that the players that have invested wisely will retire but what about those players who were not getting the big salaries do, sale cars. I beg you, use the brain that God gave you think before you do something stupid. This is my opinion and I am sticking to it.

I know that this opinion will make a lot of people angry but I have to speak my mind. Nascar is not a sport it is racing. I know that the driver's must be in great physical shape, be able to make quick decisions and drive at a very high rate of speed it is still racing. Football, basketball, hockey, golf, and baseball are sports. This statement is for one particular person, racing is not a sport it is racing like boat racing, horse racing, Indy car racing and yes Nascar. It is an activity that uses a motor therefore it is racing not a sport. This is my opinion. On a personal note, I would rather watch paint dry.

I feel it is my right to discuss the United States effort in this years Ryder Cup Event. I think that the captain did not do a very good job of forming the teams for the four ball matches and the alternative shot matches. I also thought that he used some players too much while others he did not use enough. I do not think the American athlete cares any more about events that take place against other countries. I think this because there is no money involved. A person use to take pride playing for his country but now the best players do not seem to give a hoot. This is only my opinion but I think that the United States teams should be proud of where they live, and show the rest of the world why we are the best country in the world.

I think that the best sports reporters that I have heard on television are Mike Wilbon, Bob Ryan, Woody Paige, Mitch Albom, Jay Marrotti, and Michael Smith. Their honesty on television proves that there are good sports reporters in this country. There are other good reporters but these are my favorites.

I believe that in time we will find and capture Osama Bin Laden. The day we find that low life son-of-a-bitch we should execute him on the spot, chopping him up into as many pieces as the lives that his henchman took on our home soil. This is my opinion.

I know that women come and go thru out our lives but that friendships last forever. It is a plus if a friend is a woman and a very big plus if that friend is your wife. I know that a person that has five good friends in his life, people that he can trust, then he or she is very blessed.

I know that J. Edgar Hoover was a racist. He once stated that no black man would work for the Federal Bureau of Investigation as an agent, the only way a black man could be associated with his part of the justice department was as a servant.

I think that the Nazi Party and the Ku Klux Klan should unite their efforts to further their cause. I mean they believe in the same things. Both hate Catholics, Jews, Gays, Communists and especially blacks. This would unite two groups that do not agree with the American Constitution. The Ku Klux Klan says they believe in the constitution but only if the document satisfies their desires. They believe in the original constitution which was written over 200 years ago, in order to live by that form they need to build a time machine and travel back in time to the eighteenth century. I do not believe that a person can live in this country and not defend the constitution, the entire constitution. The Nazi Party are following a man that was crazy, uneducated and a mad man that was out for one thing, him. He destroyed his own country and attempted to conquer the world besides trying to destroy an entire race of people, not just any people but gods chosen people. I truly believe that if these two factions unite, the only people that would suffer a monetary loss would be department stores that have white sheet sales after the holidays. This is my opinion. I am not trying to tell you how to live your lives. I wish that your organization did not feel how it does but I cannot change what is in your heart and mind. I only hope that some day your organization will see that it is wrong to try to destroy people that are no threat to you. The blacks did not enter this country because they wanted to move to a better place, they were kidnapped from their own country by northern slave traders and sold to southern plantation owners to harvest their crops. I think that hating a group of people because they are different from you is silly because your group would have to hate everyone. I think that your group should feel lucky that you live in a country that allows freedoms that other countries do not honor. The white race stole this country from the American Indian, was this o.k. I do not think that an American should bring harm to another American unless provoked.

The Nazi Party in this country should read books on their chosen leader. He did not like women, he was not even German, and he was Austrian. He was a sadistic man who blamed the troubles of Germany on the Jewish race. The other European countries were afraid of another world war so they allowed him to have his way until it was too late. He considered himself invincible and he tried to conquer Europe, which resulted in World War 2.

I think it is about time that the baseball hall of fame allows Pete Rose to be selected. The fans want to see this occur, maybe not his fellow players that have preceded him. I think keeping him out is an injustice to everyone. He set the all-time record for hits for pete's sake. He admitted that he bet on baseball. He even admitted that he bet on his own team. He admitted these things that he did wrong, so it is time for him to be forgiven. I also think that George Weaver and Joe Jackson be allowed to have their names placed in the hall. The commissioner of the day was an idiot for not doing some sort of investigation to see who performed their very best during the series he just took the word of people who had lost money on the games that were played. Paul Hournig and Alex Karros, were only suspended for one year from professional football for doing the exact same thing. I know that at least one of them is in the hall of fame. I think that baseball is making a tremendous error by not letting Mr. Rose and the others on the ballot. It is hard for me to believe that none of you has done anything that you are ashamed of doing. Please put his name on the ballot, then decide or let the fans make the final decision. Please remember this fact: Ty Cobb and George Herman Ruth broke the law when they played ball. They were drinking alcohol during prohibition but this is my opinion.

I believe that movie stars and athletes should be not be treated any better than the normal citizen. When they are caught using drugs or driving under the influence they should face the same penalties that everyone else must face. They should not get a slap on the wrist and sent on their way. A drug user is a drug user it does not matter if they are famous. A regular person would not receive the same treatment so why should entertainer be given special treatment is not fair. It is time for the United States Judicial System to wake up and smell the coffee. You have to be fair with everyone and treat everyone the same. This is my opinion.

I believe that the prison terms for the possession of powder and crack cocaine should be the same. The law as it is right now is racist, and wrong. Cocaine is a banned drug therefore the sentence should be the same. The law needs to be changed.

I think that in my opinion the Five GREATEST Presidents that have had the honor to serve in this position are the following:

1) Harry S. Truman- he made the decision to drop the atomic bomb to end World War 2 thus saving American lives.
2) He help establish the country of Israel
3) He integrated the Armed Services allowing blacks to serve with whites
4) He had the intestinal fortitude to dismiss General McArthur even though his decision was unpopular at the time.
5) He won reelection when he was supposed to lose. He proved he was not a quitter.
6) He paid off his creditors during the depression after filing bankruptcy.

SECOND-PRESIDENT Abraham Lincoln

1) He was the first Republican President.
2) He gave the slaves their freedom.
3) He kept the United States together no matter the cost of lives or money
4) He allowed the slaves to fight to keep the country together (slaves did fight independently)
5. He was for giving the former slaves the right to vote

THIRD-PRESIDENT George Washington

1) He was the father of our country and the first President.
2) He turned down the position of King by stating that we were not going to use that title. He said that if we were, then we fought for independence for nothing.

3) He served only two terms because that is all that a President should serve.

FOURTH-PRESIDENT Thomas Jefferson

1) He wrote the Declaration of Independence.

2) He acquired from France Louisiana and the territory that went along with the purchase. It turned out to be a very good deal.

3) He served as Ambassador to France.

FIFTH-PRESIDENT Theodore Roosevelt

1) He was a strong believer in conservation.

2) He served in the Spanish American War.

3) He won the Nobel Peace Prize for negotiating the end of the war between Russia and Japan.

These are my choices as the Five BEST Presidents. The reader might disagree but that is fine. This is only my opinion.

I do not want to leave out my Five WORST Presidents. I want to be fair.

FIRST-PRESIDENT Richard Nixon

1) I can say it in one word-Watergate. It was the biggest bone-headed blunder of all time except for President Clinton's quotation that he did not have sexual relations with that woman.

2) He was very greedy. He trusted nobody.

3) He was an alcoholic and a wife-beater. There is nothing worse than a man who takes out his frustrations on a woman. It is chicken shit and childish.

SECOND-PRESIDENT Lyndon B. Johnson

1) He appointed J. Edgar Hoover the Federal Bureau Investigation Director for life. This man was the highest government racist to hold power since before the Civil War.

2) Escalated the war in Vietnam

3) He did not seek reelection because he knew that he had wasted American lives needlessly

THIRD-PRESIDENT John F. Kennedy

1) He cheated on his wife as if it as if it was a sport.

2) He won election with the help of the mob.

3) He made a promise to the Cuban exiles to assist their retaking of their homeland from Castro, and then recanted.

4) He knew or helped in the untimely demise of Marylyn Monroe.

5) He hid his illnesses from the American public. These illnesses were life threatening.

FOURTH-PRESIDENT Ulysses S. Grant

1) Alcoholic

2) His choices for cabinet members as a whole were the most corrupt members of our country's history

3) A good soldier does not always make a good president

FIFTH-PRESIDENT James Carter

1) Weak president-no backbone

2) Allowed the embassy to be taken in Iran and allowing our personnel to be held as prisoners for 444 days.

3) He charged visitors to the White House money for food that they ate.

I think that Martin Luther King, if not assassinated would have been the first United States President in United States history. We will never know for sure. He had a dream and I think that except for a few racists and hot-heads, people would have realized his dream had merit and been given a opportunity to be president. This is my opinion.

I believe that abortion is a woman's choice. I know that some people believe that it is murder to kill a fetus, while others believe that the fetus is not a human being for the first tri-mester. I am a man so I do not know how it feels to carry a baby for nine months but I do know that if a woman feels she is not prepared to have a child then she should be able to make the decision to have the baby. People that bomb abortion clinics trying to prevent abortions are just common criminals that claim to be doing God's will. I do not think God would want those people to choose this method of prevention. I do think that if a woman does not desire to have a child, they should practice safe sex or wait until they are prepared and want a child. This is my opinion.

I think that reality shows have out stayed their welcome. Survivor, Fear Factor, Boy Meets Boy, Average Joe are only a few shows that are getting old quick. The only reality show that is any good is Last Comic Standing. It is good because the show is entertaining and funny. This is my opinion.

My favorite people from Alabama listed in order:

1) Hank Williams- best country singer that sang with his heart and soul. He left us much too early.

2) The country group Alabama- best country group ever, hailed from Fort Payne my grandparents lived there for

many years recorded such hits My Home is In Alabama, She's a Lady, Tennessee River, 40 Hour Week, just to name a few.

3) Willie Mays- I think he was the first five tool player that ever played baseball. He could run, hit, throw, and field his position and hit with power. He had a unique style when catching a fly ball. I have heard people say that he was showing off but I thought it was cool. I thank-you Willie Mays, you made baseball look fun.

4) Henry Aaron- I think you are the greatest baseball player that played the game in my life time. I believe that your record of 755 home runs will be broken by Barry Bonds but not because he is better than you, I think the reason is that the competition is not as good as the competition that you faced. You also were a five- tool player. I saw you play ball for the Braves in the 1960's. I thought you were and still are the best. I cannot fathom the torment that you suffered internally while chasing Ruth's all time record. I cannot believe that other Americans would and did send you death threats because you were about to break a record in a sport. Mister Aaron you will remain to me my favorite baseball player. I thank you for showing your style and grace on the field and your intestinal fortitude off the field. I stand a proud man and American that you played baseball and you will remain at least to me one of the greatest men of my lifetime.

5) Lynard Skynard- they were the best southern rock band ever. The song "Free bird" is the best rock song I ever

heard. The heart of the band perished in a plane crash but the band still carries on still today. The band remains very good.

6) The Rick and Bubba Show- they are as the two sexiest fat men alive. They do a talk television and radio show that discuss various subjects but with a Christian flavor added to their shows. They are very funny and if a reader of this book is ever passing through the south, give the station a listen. The show is never boring. It is a high quality show done with class.

7) My dad- he is the best person I know from Alabama. I thank him for meeting my mom and producing my sisters and I. Thanks dad.

The reason I chose Alabama was that when I was a kid my dad thought the world of Paul "Bear" Bryant. He loved Alabama football. When Alabama was playing football on television, he would call me to watch the game with him knowing I did not like his favorite team. This is the reason I chose Alabama.

I believe that prayer ought to be a part of school activities. A child that does not feel compelled to participate in this activity should not take part. He/she can just be silent. I feel that if a child is taught at an early age that it is fine to pray, this will benefit them later in life. This is my opinion.

I believe that there ought to be a national holiday for the Veterans that fought in Vietnam. The wall that honors the dead men and women is great but I feel that a holiday for the living would be good because it honors those brave people who fought in a war that the American Politicians had no desire to win. I know that it is one thing to die for your country when the result is winning but when American lives are squandered for nothing and when they return home, are treated like shit this is truly not the American way. Our government should realize this and honor these people. This is my opinion.

This is a list of my ten heroes, living and dead who have had an impact on my life:

1) My parents-they taught me to be the best person that I could be. They also raised me as if I was a normal child not a child with a disability. I participated in sports and learned to overcome my disability as best as I could. They knew that I had limitations but if I tried to succeed, I could accomplish anything that I set my mind on. They also taught me to read at an early age, thus allowing me to be able to think before I made a bad decision. This concept did not always work but it was not their fault, it was mine.

2) Jimmy Valvano- he said if a person does three things everyday, laugh, cry and to paraphrase be the best person you can be that day then you have had a good day. He also said never give up; do not ever give up no matter the odds. He left us way to early and I can say that I really miss him.

3) Lou Gehrig- he was one of the greatest baseball players that ever played the national past time. He died before his time and he left the game with dignity. We also share the same birthday 6/19. He was the reason that I liked the Yankees until George Steinbrenner became the owner.

4) Payne Stewart- he was a very nice man that played golf with a fire and passion, and he had a great sense of humor. I had the pleasure of meeting him in Chattanooga, Tennessee. He did not have to visit with me but he did, I will always remember that day. I know that he loved his family. He was another great man that left us much too early.

5) John Daly- he is a blue collar type golfer whom his fans really love. He has been through quite a bit of trials in his life. His work he does with Make-A-Wish Foundation is wonderful. He is a big hitter with a big heart. It is time for his critics to leave him alone and let him play golf I mean certain journalists should get off his back.

6) Mike Wilbon- he is a great sports journalist that in my opinion is the best sports reporter today. He also has to endure the mouth of Tony Kornheiser. I truly hope that his antics are for the show and he is not that obnoxious all the time. Mike, keep up your great work.

7) Leroy Pitt- he is my best friend. He cares about my health and tells me to shut up when I get out of line. We have had a lot of good times and I know we will have a lot more.

8) Oprah Winfrey- she is one of the most famous women today. She has her own show, her own network, and her own magazine. Most people like her for being herself. I have watched her show for many years and she has not changed to me. I admire her for the kind way that she treats people. I hope that some of her mannerisms rub off onto me.

9) My sisters- I just want to say that I love you with all my heart and soul. I do not think that I could have become the person I am today without your presence in my life. Both of you are special in different ways, yet the same in other ways. Your senses of humor are a blessing to everyone that meets either of you. I am very thankful that the two of you are related to me and I want to thank you for putting up with my crap for the last forty years.

10) Bill Jones- you are in this list for only one reason. I would not had the chance to write this book without your help getting the job in the first place.

My favorite sports are:

1) Baseball
2) Professional football
3) Golf
4) College football
5) College basketball

I really believe that sometimes I am not from the south because I do not like beer, hunting, fishing or Nascar. These things are big in the south and I do not like any of them, seems strange to me.

I think that it is wrong to speak ill of the dead but I wonder if the atheist Mrs. O'Hare said just before she was murdered "oh God please help me." It is just a thought.

I would like this to target men who abuse their wives or their children. There is no reason for a man to hit a woman. An example would be that my first wife Carol put a butcher knife to my throat and told me she was going to kill me. I laughed in her face and walked away. A woman can cuss you, hit you, and try to push your buttons to make you mad but a man can discover that it is easier to walk away than take out his frustrations on his wife. Buy a punching bag, take up a hobby, start playing a sport, get a divorce these are a few choices to do rather than going to prison. I would rather see a married man use the services of a lady of the night or find a girlfriend than to abuse a child. A man needs to seek medical help if the thought crosses his mind. A child is so vulnerable and usually very impressionable. Do not mess up their lives because you cannot control your sexual urges. I think that for a last resort; it is better for the family that you leave than cause any abuse. The wife should report any abuse to the police and file a complaint. Do not allow him to talk you out of pressing charges because if he did it once, he will repeat his action. I further believe that discipline concerning children deserves a spanking now and then, I am not talking about a beating but a spanking, and there is a difference. I received many spankings when I was a child. When I became a teenager, my punishment became different things like grounding and yard work. I remember going to my parents and begging them for a whipping instead of grounding or yard work. I think that if possible a child should be encouraged to go play outside to expand his/her mind. I believe this will help the child more than playing video games. I believe a parent should encourage their children to read a book on a subject that they are interested in such as history, romance, or whatever they find interesting. I think that a child should not play sports until they understand the sport that they are playing. Tee ball is not for the children, it is for the parents.

I believe that policemen, firemen, and school teachers should be paid a lot more money than they receive now. They perform a service to the community that is very important and vital. They put their lives on the line to protect the citizens of their respective communities. I think the next time a policeman stops you for speeding or some other moving violation, you should thank him instead of giving him/her a hard time. He is only doing his job. He should be paid well for performing his/her job. A fireman risks his life everyday. He deserves the pay that he/she receives and much, much more. The next time that you see a fireman it would be nice if they received a simple thank-you.

A school teacher deserves an increase in pay because it is their job to educate your children. It is a tireless job. This is a profession that we need bodies that are more qualified. A mind is a body part that should not be wasted. Please think with your minds and not with your wallets. I think that teachers are the spinal column, while the parents are the spine. I think that corporal punishment should be allowed in schools. A teacher has to have some control over her class. The condition of public education should be evident since discipline has been removed from the schools. I know that by removing even the threat of retribution the child has nothing to fear, thus becoming disruptive. This is my opinion.

I think that rap music is just poets that say words because they cannot sing. This genre of "music" is fine with me but instead of rapping about violence, rap about something in life that is good. This is my opinion.

This is all that I have to say about certain things. I hope I did not make anyone angry but these things were weighing on my mind.

This is my opinion and I believe that I ought to share this opinion with the readers of this book. I think that the founder of the Ku Klux Klan was John Wilkes Boothe. When this man murdered the President of the United States, this stupid act put into motion the very thing the south did not need. Lincoln was going to allow the south to return to their normal way of life without the slaves. Most of the south did not own slaves therefore; the south would have been able to begin their lives once again as farmers. The plantation owners, which were a minority, would have to pay people to harvest their crops. Lincoln's cabinet blamed the entire south for the President's death. This event was the beginning of the north's pitiful treatment of the south, which eventually caused the formation of the Ku Klux Klan. I am not saying the group would never have started but I truly believe that the assassination sped the forming of the group a lot quicker. This is my opinion.

My last opinion or thought that I would like to give is who my favorite comedians are.

1) Richard Pryor- he can tell jokes either dirty or clean but to me he is the funniest man ever to take a stage.

2) Robin Williams- he is the best at being spontaneously funny. His mind is so quick. He could make a deaf man laugh.

3) Jeff Foxworthy- he is without a doubt the funniest man from the south. His redneck jokes are priceless.

4) Sam Kinnison- he was a very talented and funny man who left this world much too early.

5) James Gregory- he is the second most humorous man from the south. My favorite routine starts out with some nut! These jokes are very good and could make a manic depressive person scream with laughter.

I hoped you have enjoyed reading my book. I would like to thank a few people who encouraged me to finish this project. I like to thank Jim, Pam, Sherman, Mr. B and my favorite bartender Linda. I want to thank you from my heart. I also want to thank a special friend from Canada, Roxanne who kept my spirits high when I got depressed when writing parts of the book.

I want to thank XYZ Battery Company for hiring me and may God bless every American.

About the Author

Pete Workman was born on June 19, 1954 in Chattanooga, Tennessee. He is the oldest of three children. He was diagnosed with cerebral palsy in his right side when he was two. His parents raised him like he didn't have a handicap. He graduated from high school in 1972 with letters in wrestling (manager) and golf. He worked at XYZ Battery Company from 1983-2000.